The Night-Walker by John Fletcher

Later revised by James Shirley

Or The Little Thief. A Comedy.

As it was presented by her Majesties Servants, at the Private House in Drury Lane

John Fletcher was born in December, 1579 in Rye, Sussex. He was baptised on December 20th.

As can be imagined details of much of his life and career have not survived and, accordingly, only a very brief indication of his life and works can be given.

Young Fletcher appears at the very young age of eleven to have entered Corpus Christi College at Cambridge University in 1591. There are no records that he ever took a degree but there is some small evidence that he was being prepared for a career in the church.

However what is clear is that this was soon abandoned as he joined the stream of people who would leave University and decamp to the more bohemian life of commercial theatre in London.

The upbringing of the now teenage Fletcher and his seven siblings now passed to his paternal uncle, the poet and minor official Giles Fletcher. Giles, who had the patronage of the Earl of Essex may have been a liability rather than an advantage to the young Fletcher. With Essex involved in the failed rebellion against Elizabeth Giles was also tainted.

By 1606 John Fletcher appears to have equipped himself with the talents to become a playwright. Initially this appears to have been for the Children of the Queen's Revels, then performing at the Blackfriars Theatre.

Fletcher's early career was marked by one significant failure; The Faithful Shepherdess, his adaptation of Giovanni Battista Guarini's Il Pastor Fido, which was performed by the Blackfriars Children in 1608.

By 1609, however, he had found his stride. With his collaborator John Beaumont, he wrote Philaster, which became a hit for the King's Men and began a profitable association between Fletcher and that company. Philaster appears also to have begun a trend for tragicomedy.

By the middle of the 1610s, Fletcher's plays had achieved a popularity that rivalled Shakespeare's and cemented the pre-eminence of the King's Men in Jacobean London. After his frequent early collaborator John Beaumont's early death in 1616, Fletcher continued working, both singly and in collaboration, until his own death in 1625. By that time, he had produced, or had been credited with, close to fifty plays.

Index of Contents

DEDICATION

To The worthily-deserving all his ingenuous Attributes William Hudson Esq.

Worthy Sir,

I Should derogate from your worth, to doubt of your pardon, and I should wrong too much your goodnesse to present the endeavours of some frothy braine to the triall of your judgement, when the More ignorant world had already condemned it; but sir, this is one of the coheirs of much admired, much lamented Fletcher, whose matchlesse Fancies are fit onely for the perusall of such as you, who have candour and knowledge so united, that there cannot be a reprive for those Poems you condemne; accept this weake Testimonie of my Service, and as yours by familiar acquaintance with them, favourably entertaine these witty conceits particularly presented unto you, by him who shall glory in nothing more than to be stiled

The Honorer of
Your Vertues,
Andrew Crook

DRAMATIS PERSONAE
Tom Lurcher
Jack Wild-Brain
Gentlemen
Justice Algripe
Frank Heartlove
Tobie
Servants
Sexton

Bell-Ringers
Boy
A Lady, Mother to Maria
Maria
Nurse
Mistriss Newlove
Women
Mistriss

Enter **TOM LURCHER** and **JACK WILD-BRAIN**.

LURCHER
Jack.

WILD-BRAIN
What wind brought thee hither?
In what old hollow tree, or rotten wall
Hast thou been like a Swallow all this winter,
Where hast thou been man?

LURCHER
Following the Plow.

WILD-BRAIN
What Plow? Thou hast no Land,
Stealing is thy own purchase.

LURCHER
The best inheritance.

WILD-BRAIN
Not in my opinion,
Thou hadst five hundred pound a year.

LURCHER
'Tis gone,
Prethee no more on't, have I not told thee,
And oftentimes, nature made all men equal,
Her distribution to each child alike;
Till labour came and thrust a new Will in,
Which I allow not: till men won a priviledge

By that they call endeavour, which indeed
Is nothing but a lawful Cosenage,
An allowed way to cheat, why should my neighbour
That hath no more soul than his Horse-keeper,
Nor bounteous faculties above a Broom-man,
Have forty thousand pounds, and I four groats;
Why should he keep it?

WILD-BRAIN
Thy old opinion still.

LURCHER
Why should that Scrivener,
That ne'er writ reason in his life, nor anything
That time e'ver gloried in, that never knew
How to keep any courtesie conceal'd,
But Noverint Universi must proclaim it,
Purchase perpetually, and I a rascal:
Consider this, why should that mouldy Cobler
Marry his Daughter to a wealthy Merchant,
And give five thousand pounds, is this good justice?
Because he has a tougher constitution;
Can feed upon old Songs, and save his money,
Therefore must I go beg?

WILD-BRAIN
What's this to thee?
Thou canst not mend it, if thou beest determin'd
To rob all like a Tyrant, yet take heed
A keener justice do not overtake thee,
And catch you in a Nooze.

LURCHER
I am no Wood-cock,
He that shall sit down frighted with that foolery
Is not worth pity, let me alone to shuffle,
Thou art for wenching.

WILD-BRAIN
For beauty I, a safe course,
No halter hangs in my way, I defie it.

LURCHER
But a worse fate, a wilful poverty,
For where thou gain'st by one that indeed loves thee,
A thousand will draw from thee, 'tis thy destiny;
One is a kind of weeping cross Jack,
A gentle Purgatory, do not fling at all,

You'll pay the Box so often, till you perish.

WILD-BRAIN
Take you no care for that sir, 'tis my pleasure,
I will imploy my wits a great deal faster
Than you shall do your fingers, and my loves,
If I mistake not, shall prove riper harvest
And handsomer, and come within less danger.
Where's thy young Sister?

LURCHER
I know not where she is, she is not worth caring for,
She has no wit.
Oh you'd be nibling with her,
She's far enough I hope, I know not where,
She's not worth caring for, a sullen thing,
She wou'd not take my counsel Jack,
And so I parted from her.

WILD-BRAIN
Leave her to her wants?

LURCHER
I gave her a little money, what I could spare,
She had a mind to th' Countrey, she is turn'd,
By this, some Farriers dairy maid, I may meet her
Riding from Market one day, 'twixt her Dorsers,
If I do, by this hand I wo'not spare
Her butter pence.

WILD-BRAIN
Thou wilt not rob thy Sister.

LURCHER
She shall account me for her Eggs and Cheeses.

WILD-BRAIN
A pretty Girl, did not old Algripe love her?
A very pretty Girl she was.

LURCHER
Some such thing,
But he was too wise to fasten; let her pass.

WILD-BRAIN
Then where's thy Mistriss?

LURCHER

Where you sha'not find her,
Nor know what stuff she is made on; no indeed Sir,
I choose her not for your use.

WILD-BRAIN
Sure she is handsome.

LURCHER
Yes indeed is she, she is very handsome, but that's all one.

WILD-BRAIN
You'll come to th' Marriage?

LURCHER
Is it to day.

WILD-BRAIN
Now, now, they are come from Church now.

LURCHER
Any great preparation,
Does Justice Algripe shew his power?

WILD-BRAIN
Very glorious, and glorious people there.

LURCHER
I may meet with him yet e're I dye as cunning as he is.

WILD-BRAIN
You may do good Tom, at the m arriage,
We have plate and dainty things.

LURCHER
Do you no harm Sir;
For yet methinks the Marriage should be mar'd
If thou maist have thy will, farewell, say nothing.

[Exit.

[Enter **GENTLEMEN.**

WILD-BRAIN
You are welcome noble friends.

FIRST GENTLEMEN
I thank you Sir,
Nephew to the old Lady, his name is Wild-Braine,

And wild his best condition.

SECOND GENTLEMEN
I have heard of him,
I pray ye tell me Sir, is young Maria merry
After her Marriage rites? does she look lively?
How does she like her man?

WILD-BRAIN
Very scurvily,
And as untowardly she prepares her self,
But 'tis mine Aunts will, that this dull mettal
Must be mixt with her to allay her handsomeness.

FIRST GENTLEMEN
Had Heartlove no fast friends?

WILD-BRAIN
His means are little,
And where those littles are, as little comforts
Ever keep company: I know she loves him,
His memory beyond the hopes of—
Beyond the Indies in his mouldy Cabinets,
But 'tis her unhandsome fate.

[Enter **HEARTLOVE**.

FIRST GENTLEMEN
I am sorry for't,
Here comes poor Frank, nay we are friends, start not Sir,
We see you'r willow and are sorry for't,
And though it be a wedding we are half mourners.

HEARTLOVE
Good Gentlemen remember not my fortunes,
They are not to be help'd by words.

WILD-BRAIN
Look up man,
A proper sensible fellow and shrink for a wench?
Are there no more? or is she all the handsomness?

HEARTLOVE
Prethee leave fooling.

WILD-BRAIN
Prethee leave thou whining,
Have maids forgot to love?

HEARTLOVE
You are injurious.

WILD-BRAIN
Let 'em alone a while, they'll follow thee.

FIRST GENTLEMEN
Come good Frank.
Forget now, since there is no remedy,
And shew a merry face, as wise men would do.

SECOND GENTLEMEN
Be a free guest, and think not of those passages.

WILD-BRAIN
Think how to nick him home, thou knowst she dotes on thee
Graff me a dainty medler on his crabstocke;
Pay me the dreaming puppy.

HEARTLOVE
Well, make your mirth, the whilst I bear my misery:
Honest minds would have better thoughts.

WILD-BRAIN
I am her Kinsman,
A n d love her well, am tender of her youth,
Yet honest Frank, before I would have that stinkard,
That walking rotten tombe, enjoy her maidenhead.

HEARTLOVE
Prethee leave mocking.

WILD-BRAIN
Prethee Frank believe me,
Go to consider, hark, they knock to dinner.

[Knock within.

Come wo't thou go?

SECOND GENTLEMEN
I prethee Frank go with us,
And laugh and dance as we do.

HEARTLOVE
You are light Gentlemen,
Nothing to weigh your hearts, pray give me leave,

I'll come and see, and take my leave.

WILD-BRAIN
We'll look for you,
Do not despair, I have a trick yet.

[Exit.

HEARTLOVE
Yes,
When I am mischievous I will believe your projects:
She is gone, for ever gone, I cannot help it,
My hopes and all my happiness gone with her.
Gone like a pleasing dream: what mirth and jollity
Raigns round about this house! how every office
Sweats with new joyes, can she be merry too?
Is all this pleasure set by her appointment?
Sure she hath a false heart then; still they grow lowder,
The old mans God, his gold, has won upon her,
(Light hearted Cordial Gold) and all my services
That offered naked truth, are clean forgotten:
Yet if she were compell'd, but it cannot be,
If I could but imagine her will mine,
Although he had her body.

[Enter **LADY** and **WILD-BRAIN.**

LADY
He shall come in.
Walk without doors o'this day, though an enemy,
It must not be.

WILD-BRAIN
You must compel him Madam.

LADY
No she shall fetch him in, Nephew it shall be so.

WILD-BRAIN
It will be fittest.

[Exit.

HEARTLOVE
Can fair Maria look again upon me?
Can there be so much impudence in sweetness?

[Enter **MARIA.**

Or has she got a strong heart to defie me?
She comes her self: how rich she is in Jewels!
Methinks they show like frozen Isicles,
Cold winter had hung on her, how the Roses
That kept continual spring within her cheeks
Are withered with the old mans dull embraces!
She would speak to me. I can sigh too Lady
But from a sounder heart: yes, and can weep too
But 'tis for you, that ever I believ'd you,
Tears of more pious value than your marriage;
You would encase your self, and I must credit you,
So much my old obedience compels from me;
Go, and forget me, and my poverty,
I need not bid you, you are too perfect that way:
But still remember that I lov'd Maria,
Lov'd with a loyal love, nay turn not from me,
I will not ask a tear more, you are bountiful,
Go and rejoyce, and I will wait upon you
That little of my life left.

MARIA
Good Sir hear me,
What has been done, was the act of my obedience
And not my will: forc'd from me by my parents,
Now 'tis done, do as I do, bear it handsomly
And if there can be more society
Without dishonor to my tye of marriage
Or place for noble love, I shall love you still,
You had the first, the last, had my will prosper'd;
You talk of little time of life: dear Frank,
Certain I am not married for eternity,
The joy my marriage brings tells me I am mortal.
And shorter liv'd than you, else I were miserable;
Nor can the gold and ease his age hath brought me
Add what I coveted, content; go with me,
They seek a day of joy, prethee let's show it,
Though it be forc'd, and by this kiss believe me
However, I must live at his command now,
I'll dye at yours.

HEARTLOVE
I have enough, I'll honor ye.

[Exeunt.

[Enter **LURCHER**.

LURCHER
Here are my trinkets, and this lusty marriage
I mean to visit, I have shifts of all sorts,
And here are a thousand wheels to set 'em working,
I am very merry, for I know this wedding
Will yield me lusty pillage: if mad Wildgoose
That debosh'd rogue keep but his antient revels,
And breed a hubbub in the house I am happy.

[Enter **BOY**.

Now what are you?

BOY
A poor distressed Boy, Sir,
Friendless and comfortless, that would intreat
Some charity and kindness from your worship,
I would fain serve, Sir, and as fain endeavour
With duteous labour to deserve the love
Of that good Gentleman should entertain me.

LURCHER
A pretty Boy, but of too mild a breeding,
Too tender, and too bashful a behaviour,
What canst thou do?

BOY
I can learn any thing,
That's good and honest, and shall please Master.

LURCHER
He blushes as he speaks, and that I like not,
I love a bold and secure confidence,
An impudence that one may trust, this boy now:
Had I instructed him, had been a Jewel,
A treasure for my use, thou canst not lye?

BOY
I would not willingly.

LURCHER
Nor thou hast not wit
To dissemble neatly?

BOY
Do you love such boys, Sir?

LURCHER

Oh mainly, mainly, I would have my Boy impudent,
Out-face all truth, yet do it piously:
Like Proteus, cast himself into all forms,
As suddain and as nimble as his thoughts,
Blanch at no danger, though it be the Gallows,
Nor make no conscience of a cosenage,
Though it be i' th' Church. Your soft, demure, still children—
Are good for nothing, but to get long Graces—
And sing Songs to dull tunes; I would keep thee
And cherish thee, hadst thou any active quality,
And be a tender Master to thy knavery,
But thou art not for my use.

BOY
Do you speak this seriously?

LURCHER
Yes indeed do I.

BOY
Would you have your boy Sir
Read in these moral mischiefs?

LURCHER
Now thou mov'st me.

BOY
And be a well-train'd youth in all activities?

LURCHER
By any means.

BOY
Or do you this to try me,
Fearing a prone nesse .

LURCHER
I speak this to make thee.

BOY
Then take me Sir, and cherish me, and love me,
You have me what you would: believe me, Sir
I can do any thing for your advantage,
I guess at what you mean; I can lie naturally,
As easily, as I can sleep Sir, and securely:
As naturally I can steal too.

LURCHER

That I am glad on,
Right heartily glad on, hold thee there, thou art excellent.

BOY

Steal any thing from any body living.

LURCHER

Not from thy Master.

BOY

That's mine own body:
And must not be.

LURCHER

The boy mends mightily.

BOY

A rich man, that like snow heaps up his moneys,
I have a kind of pious zeal to meet still;
A fool that not deserves 'em, I take pitty on,
For fear he should run mad, and so I ease him.

LURCHER

Excellent boy, and able to instruct me,
Of mine own nature just.

BOY

I scorn all hazard,
And on the edge of danger I do best, Sir,
I have a thousand faces to deceive,
And to those, twice so many tongues to flatter,
An impudence, no brass was ever tougher,
And for my conscience.

LURCHER

Peace, I have found a Jewel,
A Jewel all the Indies cannot match,
And thou sha't feel—

BOY

This title, and I ha' done, Sir;
I never can confess, I ha' that spell on me;
And such rare modesties before a Magistrate,
Such innocence to catch a Judge, such ignorance.

LURCHER

I'll learn of thee, thou art mine own, come boy,
I'll give thee action presently.

BOY
Have at you.

LURCHER
What must I call thee?

BOY
Snap, Sir.

LURCHER
'Tis most natural,
A name born to thee, sure thou art a Fairy,
Shew but thy skill, and I shall make thee happy.

[Enter **LADY, NURSE, MISTRISS, NEWLOVE, TOBIE.**

LADY
Where be these knaves? who strues up all the liveries.
Is the Bride's bed made?

TOBIE
Yes Madam and a Bell
Hung under it artificially.

LADY
Out knave, out,
Must we have 'larms now?

TOBIE
A little warning
That we may know when to begin our healths Madam;
The Justice is a kind of old Jade, Madam,
That will go merriest with a Bell.

LADY
All the house drunk.

TOBIE
This is a day of Jubile.

LADY
Are the best hangings up? and the Plate set out?
Who makes the Posset, Nurse?

NURSE
The dayrie mayd,
And she'll put that in, will make him caper:

Well Madam, well, you might ha'chose another,
A handsomer for your years.

LADY
Peace, he is rich Nurse,
He is rich, and that's beauty.

NURSE
I am sure he is rotten,
Would he had been hang'd when he first saw her. Termagant!

LADY
What an angry Quean is this, where,
Who looks to him?

TOBIE
He is very merry Madam,
M. Wild-Braine, has him in hand, ith'bottom o'th'Sellar
He sighs and tipples.

NURSE
Alass good Gentleman,
My heart's sore for thee.

LADY
Sorrow must have his course, sirra,
Give him some Sack to dry up his remembrance,
How does the Bridegroom, I was afraid of him.

NURSE
He is a trim youth to be tender of, hemp take him.
Must my sweet new blown Rose find such a winter
Before her spring be near.

LADY
Peace, peace, thou art foolish.

NURSE
And dances like a Town-top: and reels, and hobbles.

LADY
Alass, good Gentleman, give him not much wine.

TOBIE
He shall ha'none by my consent.

LADY
Are the women comforting my daughter?

NEWLOVE
Yes, yes, Madam,
And reading to her a pattern of true patience,
They read and pray for her too.

NURSE
They had need,
Ye had better marry her to her grave a great deal:
There will be peace and rest, alass poor Gentlewoman,
Must she become a Nurse now in her tenderness?
Well Madam, well my heart bleeds.

LADY
Thou art a fool still.

NURSE
Pray heaven I be.

LADY
And an old fool to be vext thus.
'Tis late she must to bed, go knave be merry,
Drink for a boy, away to all your charges.

[Exit.

[Enter **WILD-BRAIN,** and **FRANK HEARTLOVE.**

WILD-BRAIN
Do as thou wo't, but if thou dost refuse it
Thou art the stupid'st ass, there's no long arguing,
Time is too precious Frank.

HEARTLOVE
I am hot with wine.
And apt now to believe, but if thou dost this
Out of a villany, to make me wrong her,
As thou art prone enough.

WILD-BRAIN
Does she not love thee?
Did she not cry down-right e'n now to part with thee?
Had she not swounded if I had not caught her?
Canst thou have more?

HEARTLOVE
I must confess all this.

WILD-BRAIN

Do not stand prating, and misdoubting, casting,
If she go from thee now, she's lost for ever;
Now, now she's going, she that loves thee going,
She whom thou lov'st.

HEARTLOVE

Pray let me think a little.

WILD-BRAIN

There is no leisure; think when thou hast imbrac'd her
Can she imagine thou di d st ever honor her?
Ever believe thy oaths, that tamely suffer'st
An old dry ham of horse-flesh to enjoy her?
Enjoy her maiden-head; take but that from her
That we may tell posterity a man had it,
A handsome man, a Gentleman, a young man,
To save the honor of our house, the credit,
'Tis no great matter I desire.

HEARTLOVE

I hear you.

WILD-BRAIN

Free us both from the fear of breeding fools
And ophs, got by this shadow: we talk too long.

HEARTLOVE

She is going now to bed, among the women,
What opportunity can I have to meet her?

WILD-BRAIN

Let me alone, hast thou a will? speak soundly,
Speak discreetly, speak home and handsomly,
Is't not pitty, nay misery, nay infamy to leave
So rare a pie to be cut up by a raskal.

HEARTLOVE

I will go presently, now, now, I stay thee.

WILD-BRAIN

Such a dainty Doe, to be taken
By one that knows not neck-beef from a Phesant,
Nor cannot rellish Braggat from Ambrosia.
Is it not conscience?

HEARTLOVE

Yes, yes, now I feel it.

WILD-BRAIN
A meritorious thing.

HEARTLOVE
Good Father Wildgoose,
I do confess it.

WILD-BRAIN
Come then follow me.
And pluck a mans heart up, I'll lock thee privately,
Where she alone shall presently pass by,
None near to interupt thee but be sure.

HEARTLOVE
I shall be sure enough, lead on, and crown me.

WILD-BRAIN
No wringings in your mind now as you love me.

[Exit.

[Enter **LADY, MARIA, JUSTICE, GENT. NURSE, NEWLOVE.**

LADY
'Tis time you were a bed.

JUSTICE
I prethee sweet-heart
Consider my necessity, why art sad?
I must tell you a tale in your ear anon.

NURSE
Of Tom Thumb.
I believe that will prove your stiffest story.

NEWLOVE
I pitty the young wench.

FIRST GENTLEMEN
And so do I too.

SECOND GENTLEMEN
Come, old sticks take fire.

FIRST GENTLEMEN
But the plague is, he'll burn out instantly;
Give him another cup.

SECOND GENTLEMEN
Those are but flashes,
A tun of sack wonot set him high enough.
Will ye to bed?

MARIA
I must.

FIRST GENTLEMEN
Come, have a good heart,
And win him like a bowle to lye close to you,
Make your best use.

JUSTICE
Nay prethee Duck go instantly,
I'll dance a Jig or two to warm my body.

[Enter **WILD-BRAIN.**

WILD-BRAIN
'Tis almost midnight.

LADY
Prethee to bed Maria.

WILD-BRAIN
Go you afore, and let the Ladies follow,
And leave her to her thoughts a while, there must be
A time of taking leave of these same fooleries
Bewailling others maiden-heads.

LADY
Come then,
We'll wait in the next room.

JUSTICE
Do not tarry.
For if thou dost, by my troth I shall fall asleep Mall.

[Exit.

WILD-BRAIN
Do, do, and dream of Doterels, get you to bed quickly,
And let us ha'no more stir, come now, no crying,
'Tis too late now, carry your sel fe discreetly.
The old thief loves thee dearly, that's the benefit.
For the rest you must make your own play, Nay not that way,

They'll pull ye all to pieces, for your whim-whams,
Your garters and your gloves, go modestly,
And privately steal to bed, 'tis very late Mall,
For if you go by them such a new larum.

MARIA
I know not which way to avoid'em.

WILD-LOVE
This way,
This through the Cloysters: and so steal to bed,
When you are there once, all will separate
And give ye rest, I came out of my pitty
To shew you this.

MARIA
I thank you.

WILD-LOVE
Here's the keyes,
Go presently and lock the doors fast after ye,
That none shall follow.

MARIA
Good night.

WILD-LOVE
Good night sweet Cosen.
A good, and sweet night, or I'll curse thee Frank.

[Exit.

[Enter **HEARTLOVE.**

HEARTLOVE
She stays long, sure young Wildgoose has abus'd me,
He has made sport wi'me, I may yet get out again,
And I may see his face once more, I ha'foul intentions,
But they are drawn on by a fouler dealing

[Enter **MARIA.**

Hark, hark, it was the door,
Something comes this way, wondrous still and stealing
May be some walking spirit to affright me.

MARIA
Oh heaven my fortune.

HEARTLOVE
'Tis her voice, stay.

MARIA
Save me,
Bless me you better powers.

HEARTLOVE
I am no devil.

MARIA
Y'are little better to disturb me now.

HEARTLOVE
My name is Heartlove.

MARIA
Fye, fye, worthy friend.
Fye noble Sir.

HEARTLOVE
I must talk farther with ye,
You know my fair affection.

MARIA
So preserve it,
You know I am married now, for shame be civiller,
Not all the earth shall make me.

HEARTLOVE
Pray walk this way,
And if you ever lov'd me.

MARIA
Take heed Frank
How you divert that love to hate, go home prethee.

HEARTLOVE
Shall he enjoy that sweet?

MARIA
Nay pray unhand me.

HEARTLOVE
He that never felt what love was.

MARIA

Then I charge you stand farther off.

HEARTLOVE
I am tame, but let me walk wi'ye,
Talk but a minute.

MARIA
So your talk be honest,
And my untainted honor suffer not,
I'll walk a turn or two.

HEARTLOVE
Give me your hand then.

[Exit.

[Enter **WILD-BRAIN, JUSTICE, LADY, NURSE, GENTLEMEN, WOMEN, NEWLOVE.**

JUSTICE
Shee's not in her Chamber.

LADY
She is not here.

WILD-BRAIN
And I'll tell you what I dream'd.

JUSTICE
Give me a Torch.

FIRST GENTLEMEN
Be not too hasty Sir.

WILD-BRAIN
Nay let him go.
For if my dream be true he must be speedy,
He will be trickt, and blaz'd else.

NURSE
As I am a woman
I cannot blame her if she take her liberty,
Would she would make thee Cuckold, thou old bully,
A notorious cuckold for tormenting her.

LADY
I'll hang her then.

NURSE

I'll bless her then, she does justice,
Is this old stinking dogs-flesh for her dyet?

WILD-BRAIN
Prethee honest Nurse do not fret too much,
For fear I dream you'll hang your self too.

JUSTICE
The Cloister?

WILD-BRAIN
Such was my fancy, I do not say 'tis true,
Nor do I bid you be too confident.

JUSTICE
Where are the keyes, the keyes I say.

WILD-BRAIN
I dream'd she had 'em to lock her self in.

NURSE
What a devil do you mean?

[Enter **SERVANT**.

WILD-BRAIN
No harm, good Nurse be patient.

SERVANT
They are not in the window, where they use to be.

WILD-BRAIN
What foolish dreams are these?

JUSTICE
I am mad.

WILD-BRAIN
I hope so,
If you be not mad, I'll do my best to make ye.

FIRST GENTLEMEN
This is some trick.

SECOND GENTLEMEN
I smell the Wildgoose.

JUSTICE

Come Gentlemen, come quickly I beseech you,
Quick as you can, this may be your case Gentlemen.
And bring some lights, some lights.

[Exit.

WILD-BRAIN
Move faster, faster, you'll come too late else.
I'll stay behind and pray for ye, I had rather she were dishonest
Than thou shouldst have her.

[Enter **MARIA** and **HEARTLOVE.**

MARIA
Y'are most unmanly, yet I have some breath left;
And this steel to defend me, come not near me,
For if you offer but another violence,
As I have life I'll kill you, if I miss that,
Upon my own heart will I execute,
And let that fair belief out, I had of you.

HEARTLOVE
Most vertuous Maid, I have done, forgive my follies:
Pardon, O pardon, I now see my wickedness,
And what a monstrous shape it puts upon me,
On your fair hand I seal.

[Enter **JUSTICE.**

JUSTICE
Down with the door.

MARIA
We are betraid, oh Frank, Frank.

HEARTLOVE
I'll dye for ye
Rather than you shall suffer, I'll—

[Enter **OMNES.**

JUSTICE
Now enter.
Enter sweet Gentlemen, mine eyes, mine eyes,
Oh how my head a kes.

FIRST GENTLEMEN
Is it possible?

SECOND GENTLEMEN
Hold her, she sinks.

MARIA
A plot upon my honor
To poyson my fair name, a studied villany,
Farewell, as I have hope of peace, I am honest.

JUSTICE
My brains, my brains, my monstrous brains, they bud sure.

NURSE
She is gone, she is gone.

JUSTICE
A handsome riddance of her.
Would I could as easily lose her memory.

NURSE
Is this the sweet of Marriage, have I bred thee
For this reward?

FIRST GENTLEMEN
Hold, hold, he's desperate too.

JUSTICE
Be sure ye hold him fast, we'll bind him over
To the next Sessions, and if I can, I'll hang him.

HEARTLOVE
Nay then I'll live to be a terror to thee,
Sweet Virgin Rose farewell: heaven has thy beauty,
That's only fit for heaven. I'll live a little
To find the Villain out that wrought this injury,
And then most blessed soul, I'll climb up to thee.
Farewell, I feel my self another creature.

[Exit.

LADY
Oh misery of miseries.

NURSE
I told ye Madam.

LADY
Carry her in, you will pay back her portion?

JUSTICE
No not a penny, pay me back my credit,
And I'll condition wi'ye.

LADY
A sad wedding,
Her grave must be her Bridal bed: oh Mall,
Would I had wed thee to thy own content,
Then I had had thee still.

JUSTICE
I am mad, farewell,
Another wanton wife will prove a hell.

[Exeunt.

ACTUS SECUNDUS

SCÆNA PRIMA

Enter **LURCHER** and his **BOY.**

LURCHER
What hast thou done?

BOY
I have walked through all the lodgings.
A silence as if death dwelt there inhabits.

LURCHER
What hast thou seen?

BOY
Nought but a sad confusion
Every thing left in such a loose disorder
That were there twenty theeves, they would be laden.

LURCHER
'Tis very well, I like thy care, but 'tis strange
A wedding night should be so solitary.

BOY
Certainly there is some cause, some death or sickness
Is faln suddenly upon some friend,
Or some strange news is come.

LURCHER
Are they all a bed?

BOY
I think so, and sound asleep, unless it be
Some women that keep watch in a low parlor,
And drink, and weep, I know not to what end.

LURCHER
Where's all the plate?

BOY
Why lockt up in that room.
I saw the old Lady, ere she went to bed
Put up her plate, and some of the rich hangings
In a small long chest, and chains and rings are there too,
It stands close by the Table on a form.

LURCHER
'Twas a good notice, didst thou see the men.

BOY
I saw them sad too, and all take their leaves,
But what they said I was too far to hear Sir.

LURCHER
'Tis daintily discover'd, we shall certainly
Have a most prosperous night, which way?

BOY
A close one,
A back door, that the women have left open,
To go in and out to fetch necessaries,
Close on the Garden side.

LURCHER
I love thy diligence,
Wert thou not fearful?

BOY
Fearful? I'll be hang'd first.

LURCHER
Say they had spied thee.

BOY
I was then determin'd

To have cry'd down right too, and have kept 'em company,
As one that had an interest in their sadness,
Or made an errand to I know not whom Sir.

LURCHER
My dainty Boy, let us discharge, that plate
Makes a perpetual motion in my fingers,
Till I have fast hold of it.

BOY
Pray be wise Sir, do't handsomly, be not greedy,
Lets handle it with such an excellence
As if we would bring thieving into honor:
We must disguise, to fright these reverend wat ch es.

LURCHER
Still my blest Boy.

BOY
And clear the room of drunken jealousies,
The chest is of some weight, and we may make
Such noise ith carriage we may be snap'd.

LURCHER
Come open, here's a devils face.

BOY
No, no, Sir, wee'l have no shape so terrible,
We will not do the devil so much pleasure,
To have him face our plot.

LURCHER
A winding sheet then.

Boy. That's too cold a shift,
I would not wear the reward of my wickedness,
I wonder you are an old thief, and no cunninger,
Where's the long Cloak?

LURCHER
Here, here.

BOY
Give me the Turbant
And the false beard, I hear some coming this way,
Stoop, stoop, and let me sit upon your shoulders,
And now as I direct, stay, let them enter,
And when I touch move forward, make no noise.

[Enter **NURSE** and **TOBIE.**

NURSE
Oh 'tis a sad time, all the burnt wine is drunke Nic.

TOBIE
We may thank your dry chaps for't, the Canarie's gone too
No substance for a sorrowful mind to work upon,
I cannot mourn in beer, if she should walk now
As discontented spirits are wont to do.

NURSE
And meet us in the Cellar.

TOBIE
What fence have we with single beer against her?
What heart can we defie the Devil with?

NURSE
The March beer's open.

TOBIE
A fortification of March beer will do well,
I must confess 'tis a most mighty Armor,
For I presume I cannot pray.

NURSE
Why Nicolas?

TOBIE
We Coachmen have such tumbling faiths, no prayrs
Can go an even pace.

NURSE
Hold up your candle.

TOBIE
Verily Nurse, I have cry'd so much
For my young Mistriss, that is mortified,
That if I have not more sack to support me,
I shall even sleep: heiho, for another flagon;
These Burials, and Christnings are the mournful st matters,
And they ask more drink.

NURSE
Drink to a sad heart's needful.

TOBIE
Mine's ever sad, for I am ever dry Nurse.

NURSE
Methinks the light burns blew, I prethee snuff it,
There's a thief in't I think.

TOBIE
There may be one near it.

NURSE
What's that that moves there, ith' name of—Nicholas?
That thing that walks.

TOBIE
Would I had a Ladder to behold it,
Mercy upon me, the Ghost of one oth'Guard sure,
'Tis the devil by his clawes, he smels of Brimstone,
Sure he farts fire, what an Earth-quake I have in me;
Out with thy Prayer-book Nurse.

NURSE
It fell ith' the frying pan, and the Cat's eat it.

TOBIE
I have no power to pray, it grows still longer,
'Tis Steeple high now, and it sayls away Nurse.
Lets call the butler up, for he speaks Latine,
And that will daunt the devil: I am blasted,
My belly's grown to nothing.

NURSE
Fye, fye, Tobie.

[Exit.

BOY
So let them go, and whilst they are astonish'd
Let us presently upon the rest now suddenly.

LURCHER
Off, off, and up agen, when we are near the parlor,
Art sure thou knowst the Chest?

BOY
Though it were ith'dark Sir,
I can go to't.

LURCHER
On then and be happy.

[Exit.

[Enter **TOBIE**.

TOBIE
How my haunches quake, is the thing here still?
Now can I out-do any Button-maker, at his own trade,
I have fifteen fits of an Ague, Nurse, 'tis gone I hope,
The hard-hearted woman has left me alone. Nurse—
And she knows too I ha but a lean conscience to keep me company.

[Noise within.

The devil's among 'em in the Parlour sure,
The Ghost three stories high, he has the Nurse sure,
He is boyling of her bones now, hark how she whistles:
There's Gentlewomen within too, how will they do?
I'll to the Cook, for he was drunk last night,
And now he is valiant, he is a kin to th'devil too,
And fears no fire.

[Enter **LURCHER** and **BOY**.

LURCHER
No light?

BOY
None left Sir,
They are gone, and carried all the candles with 'em,
Their fright is infinite, let's make good use on't,
We must be quick sir, quick, or the house will rise else.

LURCHER
Was this the Chest?

BOY Yes, yes.

LURCHER
There was two of 'em.
Or I mistake.

BOY
I know the right, no stay Sir,
Nor no discourse, but to our labor lustily,
Put to your strength and make as little noise,

Then presently out at the back door.

LURCHER
Come Boy.
Come happy child and let me hug thy excellence.

[Exit.

[Enter **WILD-BRAIN**.

WILD-BRAIN
What thousand noises pass through all the rooms!
What cryes and hurries! sure the devil's drunk.
And tumbles through the house, my villanies
That never made me apprehend before
Danger or fear, a little now molest me;
My Cosens death sits heavy o'my conscience,
Would I had been half hang'd when I hammer'd it.
I aim'd at a living divorce, not a burial
That Frank might have had some hope: hark still
In every room confusion, they are all mad,
Most certain all stark mad within the house,
A punishment inflicted for my lewdness,
That I might have the more sense of my mischief,
And run the more mad too, my Aunt is hang'd sure,
Sure hang'd her self, or else the fiend has fetch'd her.
I heard a hundred cryes, the Devil, the Devil,
Th e n roaring, and then tumbling, all the chambers
Are a meer Babel, or another Bedlam.
What should I think? I shake my self too:
Can the Devil find no time, but when we are merry,
Here's something comes.

[Enter **NEWLOVE**.

NEWLOVE
Oh that I had some company,
I care not what they were, to ease my misery,
To comfort me.

WILD-BRAIN
Whose that?

NEWLOVE
Again? nay then receive—

WILD-BRAIN
Hold, hold I am no fury.

The Merchants wife.

NEWLOVE
Are ye a man? pray heaven you be.

WILD-BRAIN
I am.

NEWLOVE
Alass I have met Sir
The strangest things to night.

WILD-BRAIN
Why do you stare.

NEWLOVE
Pray comfort me, and put your candle out,
For if I see the spirit again I dye for't.
And hold me fast, for I shall shake to pieces else.

WILD-BRAIN
I'll warrant you, I'll hold ye,
Hold ye as tenderly; I have put the light out,
Retire into my Chamber, there I'll watch wi'ye,
I'll keep you from all frights.

NEWLOVE
And will ye keep me.

WILD-BRAIN
Keep you as secure Lady.

NEWLOVE
You must not wrong me then, the devil will have us.

WILD-BRAIN
No, no, I'll love you, then the devil will fear us.
For he fears all that love, pray come in quickly,
For this is the malicious house he walks in,
The hour he blasts sweet faces, lames the limbs in,
Depraves the senses, now within this half hour
He will have power to turn all Citizens wives
Into strange Creatures, Owles, and long-tail'd Monkeys,
Jayes, Pies, and Parrots, quickly, I smell his brimstone.

NEWLOVE
It comes agen I am gone shift for your self Sir.

[Exit.

WILD-BRAIN
Sure this whole night is nothing but illusion,
Here's nothing comes, all they are mad, damn'd devil
To drive her back again, 't had been thy policy
To have let us alone, we might have done some fine thing
To have made thy hel-hood laugh, 'tis a dainty wench,
If I had her again, not all your fellow goblins,
Nor all their clawes should scratch her hence, I'll stay still,
May be her fright will bring her back again,
Yet I will hope.

[Enter **TOBIE**.

TOBIE
I can find no bed, no body, nor no chamber,
Sure they are all ith'Cellar, and I cannot find that neither,
I am led up and down like a tame ass, my light's out
And I grope up and down like blind-man-buffe,
And break my face, and break my pate.

WILD-BRAIN
It comes again sure
I see the shadow, I'll have faster hold now,
Sure she is mad, I long to lye with a mad-woman,
She must needs have rare new tricks.

TOBIE
I hear one whisper
If it be the devil now to allure me into his clutches,
For devils have a kind of tone like crickets.

WILD-BRAIN
I have a glimpse of her guise, 'tis she would steal by me,
But I'll stand sure.

TOBIE
I have but a dram of wit left,
And that's even ready to run, oh for my bed now.

WILD-BRAIN
She nam'd a bed, I like that, she repents sure,
Where is she now?

TOBIE
Who's that?

WILD-BRAIN
Are you there, In, In, In presently.

TOBIE
I feel his talents through me,
'Tis an old haggard devil, what will he do with me?

WILD-BRAIN
Let me kiss thee first, quick, quick.

TOBIE
A leacherous Devil.

WILD-BRAIN
What a hairy whore 'tis, sure she has a muffler.

TOBIE
If I should have a young Satan by him, for I dare not deny him,
In what case were I? who durst deliver me?

WILD-BRAIN
'Tis but my fancy, she is the same, in quickly,
gently my Sweet girl.

TOBIE
Sweet devil be good to me.

[Exeunt.

[Enter **LURCHER** and **BOY.**

LURCHER
Where's my love, Boy.

BOY
She's coming with a Candle
To see our happy prize.

LURCHER
I am cruel weary.

BOY
I cannot blame ye, plate is very heavy
To carry without light or help.

LURCHER
The fear too
At every stumble to be discover'd boy,

At every cough to raise a Constable,
Well, we'll be merry now.

BOY
Things compass'd without fear or eminent danger,
Are too luxurious sir to live upon.
Money and wealth got thus are as full venture,
And carry in their nature as much merit
As his, that digs 'em out 'oth' mine, they last too
Season'd with doubts and dangers most delitiously,
Riches that fall upon us are too ripe,
And dull our appetites.

LURCHER
Most learned child.

[Enter **MISTRISS**.

MISTRISS
Y'are welcome, where have you left it.

LURCHER
In the next room, hard by.

MISTRISS
Is it plate all.

LURCHER
All, all, and Jewels, I am monstrous weary,
Prethee let's go to bed.

MISTRISS
Prethee lets see it first.

LURCHER
To morrow's a new day sweet.

MISTRISS
Yes to melt it,
But let's agree to night, how it shall be handled,
I'll have a new gown.

LURCHER
'Shat have any thing.

MISTRISS
And such a riding suit as Mistress Newloves:
What though I be no Gentlewoman born,

I hope I may atchieve it by my carriage.

LURCHER
Thou sayst right.

MISTRISS
You promis'd me a horse too, and a lackquay.

LURCHER
Thou shalt have horses six, and a postilion.

MISTRISS
That will be stately sweet heart, a postilion.

LURCHER
Nay, we'll be in fashion; he shall ride before us
In winter, with as much dirt would dampe a musket;
The inside of our coach shall be of scarlet.

MISTRISS
That will be dear.

LURCHER
There is a dye projecting
Will make it cheap, wench, come thou shalt have any thing.

MISTRISS
Where is this chest, I long, sweet, to behold
Our Indies.

BOY
Mistress lets melt it first, and then 'tis fit
You should dispose it, then 'tis safe from danger.

MISTRISS
I'll be a loving Mistress to my boy too.
Now fetch it in and lets rejoyce upon't.

BOY
Hold your light Mistress, we may see to enter.

MISTRISS
Ha what's here? call you this a chest?

BOY
We ha mist Sir.
Our haste and want of light made us mistake.

MISTRISS

A very Coffin.

LURCHER

How! a Coffin? Boy, 'tis very like one.

BOY

The devil ow'd us a shame, and now he has paid us.

MISTRISS

Is this your Treasure?

BOY

Bury me alive in't.

LURCHER

It may be there is no room.

MISTRISS

Nay, I will search it:
I'll see what wealth's within,—a womans face,
And a fair womans.

BOY

I cannot tell sir,
Belike this was the sadness that possest 'em;
The plate stood next, I'm sure.

LURCHER

I shake, I shake Boy, what a cold sweat—

BOY

This may work, what will become on's Sir?

MISTRISS

She is cold, dead cold: de'e find 'your conscience,
De'e bring your Gillians hither—nay, she's punish'd,
You conceal'd love's cas'd up?

LURCHER

'Tis Maria, the very same, the Bride, new horror!

MISTRISS

These are fine tricks, you hope she's in a sound
But I'll take order she shall ne'r recover
To bore my Nose, come, take her up and bury her
Quickly, or I'll cry out; take her up instantly.

LURCHER

Be not so hasty fool, that may undo us;
We may be in for murther so; be patient,
Thou seest she's dead, and cannot injure thee.

MISTRISS

I am sure she shall not.

BOY

Be not, Sir, dejected,
Too much a strange mistake! this had not been else,
It makes me almost weep to think upon't.

LURCHER

What an unlucky thief am I!

MISTRISS

I'll no considering, either bestir your self, or—

LURCHER

Hold.

MISTRISS

Let it not stay, to smell then, I will not
Indure the stink of a Rival.

LURCHER

Would 'twere there again.

BOY

We must bury her.

LURCHER

But were o'th sudden, or with what providence,
That no eyes watch us.

MISTRISS

Take a Spade and follow me,
The next fair ground we meet, make the Church-yard;
As I live, I'll see her lodg'd.

[Exit.

LURCHER

It must be so,
How heavy my heart is, I ha no life left.

BOY

I am past thinking too, no understanding,
That I should miss the right Chest.

LURCHER
The happy Chest.

BOY
That, which I saw and markt too.

LURCHER
Well passion wo'not help us,
Had I twenty falls for this!

BOY
'Twas my fault sir.
And twenty thousand fears for this, oth'devil,
Now could I curse, well, we have her now,
And must dispose her.

[Enter **MISTRISS**.

MISTRISS
Hang both for two blind buzzards, here's a Spade
Quickly or I'll call the neighbors.
There's no remedy,
Would the poor hungry prisoners had this pastie.

[Exeunt.

[Enter **JUSTICE,** and a **SERVANT** with a light.

SERVANT
'Twas a strange mischance Sir.

JUSTICE
Mischance, sayst? No 'twas happiness to me,
There's so much charge say'd, I have her portion,
I'll marry twenty more on such conditions.

SERVANT
Did it not trouble you Sir,
To see her dead?

JUSTICE
Not much, I thank my conscience;
I was tormented till that happen'd, furies
Were in my brain to think my self a Cuckold
At that time of the night:

When I come home, I charge you shut my doors,
Locks, bolts, and bars, are little enough to secure me.

SERVANT
Why, and please you?

JUSTICE
Fool to ask that question;
To keep out women, I expect her Mother
Will visit me with her clamors, oh I hate
Their noise, and do abhor the whole sex heartily;
They are all walking Devils, Harpyes: I will study
A week together how to rail sufficiently,
Upon 'em all, and that I may be furnish'd,
Thou shalt buy all the railing Books and Ballads,
That Malice hath invented against women,
I will read nothing else, and practise 'em,
Till I grow fat with curses.

SERVANT
If you'll go
To th'charge, let me alone to find you Books.

JUSTICE
They come neer us.

SERVANT
Whats that?

JUSTICE
Where? hold up the Torch Knave

SERVANT
Did you hear nothing, 'tis a—

JUSTICE
Why dost make a stand?

SERVANT
Whats that?

JUSTICE
Where, where, dost see any thing?
We are hard by the Church-yard, and I was never
Valiant at midnight in such irksome places;
They say Ghosts walk sometimes, hark, de'e hear nothing?

[Enter **LURCHER, BOY,** and **MISTRISS.**

MISTRISS
No farther, dig here, and lay her in quickly.

LURCHER
What light is that Boy, we shall be discover'd;
Set the Coffin up an end, and get behind me,
There's no avoiding.

BOY
Oh!

JUSTICE
Where's that groan? I begin to be afraid.

SERVANT
What shall we do Sir?

JUSTICE
We are almost at home now, thou must go forward,
Perhaps 'twas my imagination.

LURCHER
'Tis he?

BOY
I know him too, let me alone.

SERVANT
Oh Sir, a Ghost, the very Ghost of Mistress Bride,
I have no power to run away.

JUSTICE
Cursed Ghost, bless me, preserve me,
I do command thee what so ere thou art,
I do conjure thee leave me; do not fright me;
If thou beest a devil vex me not so soon,
If thou beest
The spirit of my wife.

BOY
Thy Wife.

JUSTICE
I shall be tormented.

BOY
Thy abus'd wife, that cannot peaceably

Enjoy her death, thou hast an evil conscience.

JUSTICE
I know it.

BOY
Among thy other sins which black thy soul,
Call to thy mind thy vow made to another,
Whom thou hast wrong'd, and make her satisfaction
Now I am dead, thou perjur'd man: or else
A thousand black tormentors shall pursue thee,
Untill thou leap into eternal flames;
Where gold which thou ador e 'st here on earth
Melted, the fiends shall powre into thy throat;
For this time pass, go home and think upon me.

LURCHER
Away.

SERVANT
There are more spirits.

JUSTICE
Thank you dear wife,
I'll bestow twenty nobles of a Tomb for thee,
Thou shalt not walk and catch cold after death. They go Backward in.

LURCHER
So, so, they'r gone, 'twas my ingenious rascal:
But how dost thou know he made vows to another?

BOY
I over-heard the woman talk to night on't;
But now let's lose no time Sir, pray lets bury
This Gentlewoman, where's my Mistress?

[Enter **MISTRISS**.

MISTRISS
Here I durst not tarry.

LURCHER
We ha so cosen'd the old forty i'th hundred,
And the devil hinder him not, he'll go a pilgrimage;
But come, about our business, set her down again.

MARIA
Oh!

LURCHER
She groans, ha.

MARIA
Oh!

LURCHER
Again, she stirs.

MISTRISS
Lets fly, or else we shall be torn in pieces.

LURCHER
And you be good at that, bury your self,
Or let the Sexton take ye for his fee,
Away boy.

[Exit.

MARIA
I am very cold, dead cold;
Where am I? What's this? a Coffin? where have I been?
Mercy defend me: Ha? I do remember
I was betray'd, and swounded, my heart akes,
I am wondrous hungry too, dead bodies eat not;
Sure I was meant for burial, I am frozen;
Death, 'like a cake of Ice dwells round about me;
Darkness spreads o're the world too, where? what path?
Best providence direct me.

[Exit.

ACTUS TERTIUS

SCÆNA PRIMA

Enter **LADY, WILD-BRAIN, WOMEN, TOBIE.**

LADY
Thou art the most unfortunate fellow.

WILD-BRAIN
Why Aunt what have I done?

LADY

The most malicious varlet,
Thy wicked head never at rest, but hammering,
And ha t ching hellish things, and to no purpose,
So thou mayst have thy base will.

WILD-LOVE
Why do you rail thus?
Cannot a scurvy accident fall out,
But I must be at one end on't?

LADY
Thou art at both ends.

WILD-LOVE
Cannot young sullen wenches play the fools
And marry, and dye, but I must be the agent?
All that I did (and if that be an injury,
Let the world judge it) was but to perswade her,
And (as I take it) I was bound to it too,
To make the reverend coxcombe her husband Cuckold:
What else could I advise her? was there harm i'this?
You are of years, and have run through experience,
Would you be content if you were young again,
To have a continual cough grow to your pillow?
A rottenness, that vaults are perfumes to;
Hang in your roof, and like a fog infect you?
Anointed hammes, to keep his hinges turning,
Reek ever in your nose, and twenty night caps,
With twenty several sweats?

TOBIE
Some Jew, some Justice,
A thousand heathen smels to say truth Madam,
And would you mellow my young pretty Mistriss
In such a mis-ken?

LADY
Sirra,
Where's the body of my Girl?

WILD-LOVE
I know not,
I am no Conjurer, you may look the body,
I was like to be stol'n away my self, the Spirit
Had like to ha surpris'd me in the shape of a woman,
Of a young woman, and you know those are dangerous.

TOBIE

So had I Madam, simply though I stand here,
I had been ravish'd too: I had twenty Spirits,
In every corner of the house a Fiend met me.

LADY

You lye like Raskals,
Was Mistriss Newlove such a spirit Sir?
To fright your worship;
Well, I discharge you Sir, y'are now at liberty,
Live where you please, and do what pranks you fancy,
You know your substance: though you are my Nephew,
I am no way bound Sir to protect your mischief;
So fare you well.

WILD-LOVE

Farewell good Aunt, I thank you,
Adiew honest Nick, the devil if he have power,
Will persecute your old bones, for this Marriage,
Farewell Mistress Win.

TOBIE

And shall we part with dry lips?
Shall we that have been fellow devils together
Flinch for an old womans fart?

WILD-LOVE

'Tis a fine time a night too, but we must part Nick.

TOBIE

Shall we never ring again? ne'r toss the tenor,
And roul the changes in a Cup of Clarret?
You shall not want what ere I lay my hands on,
As I am sure Automedon the Coachman,
Shall be distributed; bear up, I say, hang sorrow,
Give me that bird abroad that lives at pleasure,
Sam the Butler's true, the Cook a reverend Trojan,
The Faulkner shall sell his Hawks, and swear they were rotten,
There be some wandring spoons, that may be met with,
I'll pawn a Coach horse, peace, utter no sentences.
The har nesse shall be us'd in our wars also;
Or shall I drive her (tell me but your will now,
Say but the word) over some rotten bridg,
Or by a Marl-pit side, she may slip in daintily,
Let me alone for my self.

WILD-LOVE

No, no, farewell Toby,
Farewell spiny Nicholas, no such thing,

There be ways i'the world, if you see me
A day or two hence, may be wee'l crack a quart yet,
And pull a bell, commend to the houshold;
Nay, cry not Toby, 'twill make thy head giddy.

TOBIE
Sweet Master Wild-Brain.

WILD-LOVE
No more Toby, go the times may alter—
But where's the coarse of my dead cosen,
(If she be dead) I hop'd 'thad but dissembled
That sits heavy here: Toby, honest Toby,
Lend me thy Lanthorn, I forgot 'twas dark,
I had need look to my ways now.

TOBIE
Take a lodging with me to night in the Stable,
And ride away to morrow with one of the horses,
Next your heart, pray do.

WILD-LOVE
No, good night good neighbor Toby, I will wander,
I scorn to submit my self, ere I have rambled,
But whither, or with what, that's more material;
No matter, and the worst come, it is but stealing,
And my Aunt wo'not see me hang'd for her own credit,
And farewel in a Halter costs me nothing.

[Exit.

[Enter **HEARTLOVE**.

HEARTLOVE
The night, and all the evil the night covers,
The Goblins, Haggs, and the black spawn of darkness,
Cannot fright me: no death, I dare thy cruelty.
For I am weary both of life and light too;
Keep my wits heaven, they say spirits appear
To melancholy minds, and the graves open,
I would fain see the fair Maria's shadow,
But speak unto her spirit e'er I dyed,
But ask upon my knees a mercy from her;
I was a villain, but her wretched kinsman,
That set his plot, shall with his heart-blood satisfie
Her injur'd life and honor, what light's this?

[Enter **WILD-BRAIN** with a Lanthorn.

WILD-BRAIN

It is but melancholy walking thus;
The Tavern doors are baracado'd too,
Where I might drink till morn in expectation;
I cannot meet the Watch neither; nothing in
The likeness of a Constable, whom I might,
In my distress, abuse, and so be carried,
For want of other lodging, to the Counter.

HEARTLOVE

'Tis his voice, Fate, I thank thee.

WILD-BRAIN

Ha, who's that, and thou be'st a man speak?
Frank Heartlove, then I bear my destinies,
Thou art the man of all the world I wish'd for;
My Aunt has turn'd me out a doors, she has,
At this unchristian hour, and I do walk,
Methinks like Guido Faux with my dark Lanthorn,
Stealing to set the Town a fire; i'th' Countrey
I should be tane for William o' the Wispe,
Or: Robin Good-fellow, and how dost Frank?

HEARTLOVE

The worse for you.

WILD-BRAIN

Come, tha'rt a fool, art going to thy lodging?
I'll lie with thee to night, and tell thee stories,
How many devils we ha met withal;
Our house is haunted Frank, whole legions,
I saw fifty for my share.

HEARTLOVE

Didst not fright 'em?

WILD-BRAIN

How; fright 'em? no, they frighted me sufficiently.

HEARTLOVE

Thou hadst wickedness enough to make them stare,
And be afraid o' thee, malicious devil;
And draw thy sword, for by Maria's soul;
I will not let thee scape to do more mischief.

WILD-BRAIN

Thou art mad, what dost mean?

HEARTLOVE

To kill thee, nothing else will ease my anger,
The injury is fresh, I bleed withal,
Nor can that word express it, theres no peace in't,
Nor must it be forgiven, but in death;
Therefore call up thy valour, if thou'st any.
And summon up thy spirits to defend thee;
Thy heart must suffer for thy damn'd practises,
Against thy noble cosin, and my innocence.

WILD-BRAIN

Hold, hear a word; did I do any thing
But for your good, that you might have her,
That in that desperate time I might redeem her,
Although with shew of loss.

HEARTLOVE

Out ugly villain,
Fling on her the most hated name of whore
To the worlds eye, and face it out in courtesie,
Bring him to see't, and make me drunk to attempt it.

[Enter **MARIA**.

MARIA

I hear some voices this way.

HEARTLOVE

No more, if you can pray, do it as you fight.

MARIA

What new frights oppose me? I have heard that tongue.

WILD-BRAIN

'Tis my fortune.
You could not take me in a better time, Sir,
I ha nothing to lose but the love I lent thee,
My life my sword protect.

MARIA

I know 'em both, but to prevent their ruines,
Must not discover—stay men most desperate;
The mischief you are forward to commit
Will keep me from my grave, and tie my spirit
To endless troubles else.

WILD-BRAIN

Ha, 'tis her Ghost.

HEARTLOVE
Maria?

MARIA
Hear me both, each wound you make
Runs through my soul, and is a new death to me,
Each threatening danger will affright my rest;
Look on me Heartlove, and my kinsman view me;
Was I not late in my unhappy marriage,
Sufficient miserable? full of all misfortunes?
But you must add, with your most impious angers,
Unto my sleeping dust this insolence?
Would you teach time to speak eternally
Of my disgraces; make Records to keep 'em,
Keep them in brass? fight then, and kill my honor;
Fight deadly both, and let your bloody swords,
Through my reviv'd, and reeking infamy
(That never shall be purg'd) find your own ruines:
Heartlove, I lov'd thee once, and hop'd again
In a more blessed love to meet thy spirit,
If thou kill'st him, thou art a murtherer,
And murther shall never inherit heaven:
My time is come, my concealed grave expects me,
Farewel, and follow not, your feet are bloody,
And will pollute my peace: I hope they are melted,
This is my way sure.

[Exit.

HEARTLOVE
Stay blessed soul.

WILD-LOVE
Would she had come sooner, and ha sav'd some blood.

HEARTLOVE
Dost bleed?

WILD-BRAIN
Yes certainly, I can both see and feel it.

HEARTLOVE
Now I well hope it is not dangerous;
Give me thy hand, as farre as honor guides me,
I'll know thee again.

WILD-BRAIN

I thank thee heartily;
I know not where to get a Surgeon;
This vision troubles me, sure she is living,
And I was foolish blind, I could not find it;
I bleed apace still, and my heart grows heavy,
If I go far I faint, I'll knock at this house,
They may be charitable, would 'twere perfect day.

[Enter **MISTRISS**.

MISTRISS

'Tis not he: What would you, Sir?

WILD-BRAIN

I would crave a little rest Lady,
And for my hurts some Surgerie, I am a Gentleman
That fortune of a fight—

MISTRISS

A handsome Gentleman,
Alas he bleeds, a very handsome Gentleman.

WILD-BRAIN

A sweet young wench, beshrew my heart a fair one;
Fortune has made me some recompence.

MISTRISS

Pray come in, the air is hurtful for you,
Pray let me lead you, I'll have a bed for you presently,
I'll be your Surgeon too, alas sweet Gentleman.

WILD-BRAIN

I feel no hurts, the morning comes too fast now.

MISTRISS

Softly, I beseech you.

[Exit.

[Enter **LADY** and **TOBIE.**

TOBIE

He is not up yet Madam, what meant you
To come forth so early?

LADY

You blockhead;

Your eyes are sow'd up still, they cannot see
When it is day: oh my poor Maria;
Where be the women?

TOBIE
They said they would follow us.

LADY
He shall not laugh thus at my misery,
And kill my child, and steal away her body,
And keep her portion too.

TOBIE
Let him be hang'd for't,
You have my voice.

LADY
These women not come yet?
A Son-in-law, I'll keep a Conjurer,
But I'll find out his knavery.

TOBIE
Do, and I'll help him.
And if he were here, this whip should conjure him,
Here's a Capias, and it catch hold on's breech,
I'de make him soon believe the Devil were there.

LADY
An old Usurer.

TOBIE
He married the money, that's all he lookt for;
For your daughter, let her sink or swim.

LADY
I'll swim him;
This is his house, I wonder they stay thus,
That we might rail him out on's wits.

TOBIE
They'll come,
Fear not Madam, and bring clappers with 'em,
Or some have lost their old wont, I have heard,
No disparagement to your Ladyship, some o' their tongues
Like Tom-a-Lincoln, three miles off.

LADY
Oh fie,

How tedious are they?

TOBIE
What and we lost no time,
You and I shall make a shift to begin with him,
And tune our Instruments till the Consort come
To make up the full noise, I'll knock.

JUSTICE
Who's that rapt so saucily?

TOBIE
'Tis I, Toby, come down, or else we'll fetch you down,
Alas, this is but the Saunce bell, here's a Gentlewoman
Will ring you another peal, come down, I say.

JUSTICE
Some new fortifications, look to my doors,
Put double barrs, I will not have her enter,
Nor any of her Tribe, they come to terrifie me:
Keep out her tongue too, if you can.

LADY
I hear you,
And I will send my tongue up to your worship,
The eccho of it shall flye o'er the street;
My Daughter that thou killedst with kindness (Jew)
That thou betrayedst to death, thou double Jew,
And after stol'st her body.

TOBIE
Jew's too good for him.

JUSTICE
I defie you both;
Thy daughter plaid the villain and betraid me.
Betrai'd my honor.

LADY
Honor, Rascal,
And let that bear an action, I'll try it with thee,
Honor?

TOBIE
Oh Reprobate!

LADY
Thou musty Justice,

Buy an honourable halter and hang thy self.

TOBIE
A worshipful ropes end is too good for him.

LADY
Get honor that way, thou wot die a dog else.

TOBIE
Come and be whipt first.

LADY
Where is her Portion.

[Enter **NURSE** and **WOMEN.**

JUSTICE
Where I'll keep it safely.

NURSE
Traitor, thou shall not keep it.

JUSTICE
More of the kennel? put more bolts to th' doors there,
And arm your selves, hell is broke loose upon us.

TOBIE
I am glad y'are come, we'll blow the house down.

LADY
Oh Nurse, I have such cause—

WOMEN
Villain, viper, although you had no cause, we are bound
To help.

NURSE
Yes, and believe, we come not here to examine,
And if you please we'll fire the house.

JUSTICE
Call the Constable.

TOBIE
A charitable motion, fire is comfortable.

LADY
No, no, we'll only let him know our minds,

We will commit no outrage, he's a Lawyer.

JUSTICE
Give me my Musket.

LADY
Where's my daughters body,
That I may bury it?

WOMEN
Speak, or we'll bury thee.

NURSE
Alive, we'll bury thee, speak old Iniquity.

TOBIE
Bury him alive by all means for a testimony.

JUSTICE
Their voices make my house reel, oh for Officers,
I am in a dream, thy daughters spirit
Walkes a nights, and troubles all the neigh bours:
Go hire a Conjurer, I'll say no more.

LADY
The Law shall say more.

WOMEN & NURSE
We are Witnesses,
And if thou be'st not hang'd—

[Enter **LURCHER** and **BOY.**

LURCHER
Buy a Book of good manners,
A short Book of good manners.

BOY
Buy a ballad, a ballad of the maid was got with child.

TOBIE
That might ha been my case last night,
I'll ha't, what e'er it cost me.

BOY
A ballad of the Witches hang'd at Ludlow.

TOBIE

I will have that too;
There was an Aunt of mine, I think amongst 'em,
I would be glad to hear her Testament.

LURCHER
A new Book of Women.

JUSTICE
The thunder's laid, how they stare at him.

LURCHER
A new Book of Fools, a strange Book,
Very strange fools.

JUSTICE
I'll owe thee a good turn, whate'er thou art.

LURCHER
A Book of Walking Spirits.

JUSTICE
That I like not.

TOBIE
Nor I, they walk'd me the Fools Morris.

LURCHER
A Book of Wicked Women.

JUSTICE
That's well thought on.

LURCHER
Of rude, malicious Women, of proud Women,
Of scolding Women, we shall ne'er get in.

BOY
A ballad of wrong'd Maids.

LADY
I'll buy that.

LURCHER
A little, very little Book,
Of good and godly Women, a very little one,
So little you may put it in a Nutshel.

TOBIE

With a small print that no body can read it.

NURSE
Peace sirrah, or I'll tear your Books.

JUSTICE
Open the door and let him in, I love him.

LURCHER
A Book of evil Magistrates.

LADY
I marry d'ye hear that Justice.

LURCHER
And their eviller wives,
That wear their Places in their Petticoats.

JUSTICE
D'ye hear that Lady.

BOY
A Book new printed against Playing,
Dancing, Masking, May-poles; a zealous Brothers Book,
And full of Fables.

LURCHER
Another Book of Women, of mad women,
Women that were born in March.

[Exit.

LADY
Are you got in?
We would ha pull'd your knaves hide else; this fellow
Was sent to abuse us, but we shall have time
To talk more with this Justice.

JUSTICE
Farewel Madam, as you like this, come visit me agen,
You and your treble strings, now scold your hearts out—

WOMEN
Shall he carry it thus away?

NURSE
Go to the Judge, and what you'll have us swear—

LADY
I thank ye heartily,
I'll keep that for the last, I will go home,
And leave him to his Conscience for a while,
If it sleep long, I'll wake it with a vengeance.

[Exit.

[Enter **SERVANTS**.

FIRST SERVANT
What book has he given thee?

SECOND SERVANT
A dainty book, a book of the great Navy,
Of fifteen hundred ships of Cannon-proof,
Built upon Whales to keep their keels from sinking:
And Dragons in 'em, that spit fire ten mile;
And Elephants that carry goodly Castles.

FIRST SERVANT
Dost thou believe it?

SECOND SERVANT
Shall we not believe Books in print?

FIRST SERVANT
I have John Taylors book of Hempseed too,
Which for two lines I hapned on by chance,
I reverence.

SECOND SERVANT
I prethee what are they?

FIRST SERVANT
They are so pat upon the time, as if
He studied to answer the late Histriomastix,
Talking of change and transformations,
That wittily, and learnedly he bangs him,
So many a Puritans ruff, though starch'd in print,
Be turn'd to Paper, and a Play writ in't
A Play in the Puritans ruff? I'll buy his Works for't,
And confute Horace with a Water Poet:
What hast there a Ballad too?

SECOND SERVANT
This? This is a piece of Poetry indeed;

[He sings; **JUSTICE** cries within.

What noise is that?

FIRST SERVANT
Some cry i th' streets; prethee sing on. Sing s again.

SECOND SERVANT
Agen, dost not hear? 'tis i'th' house certainly?

FIRST SERVANT
'Tis a strange noise! and has a tang o'th' Justice.

SECOND SERVANT
Let's see!

[Exit.

[Enter the **SERVANTS** bringing in their **MASTER** bound and gagg'd.

FIRST SERVANT
Untie his feet, pull out his gagg, he will choak else;
What desperate rogues were these.

SECOND SERVANT
Give him fresh air.

JUSTICE
I will never study books more:
I am undone, these villains have undone me.
Rifled my Desk, they have undone me learnedly:
A fire take all their Books, I'll burn my Study:
Where were you rascals when the villains bound me,
You could not hear?

FIRST SERVANT
He gave us Books, Sir, dainty Books to busie us;
And we were reading, in that which was the Brew-house;
A great way off, we were singing Ballads too;
And could not hear.

JUSTICE
This was a precious thief,
A subtle trick to keep my servants safe.

SECOND SERVANT
What ha you lost Sir?

JUSTICE

They ransack'd all before my face, and threatned
To kill me if I cough'd, they have a chain,
My rings, my box of casting gold, my purse too.
They robb'd me miserably: but that which most grieves me,
They took away some Writings; 'twas a rogue
That knew me, and set on by the old Lady,
I will indite her for't.

FIRST SERVANT

Shall we pursue 'em?

JUSTICE

Run, run, cursed raskals,
I am out of my wits, let not a creature in,
No not with necessaries.

SECOND SERVANT

We shall be starv'd.

JUSTICE

I'll buy my meat at window as they pass by;
I wonot trust my Scrivenor, he has books too;
And bread I'll ha flung up; I charge ye all
Burn all the books i'th' house.

FIRST SERVANT

Your little Prayer Book?

JUSTICE

I'll never pray agen, I'll have my doors
Made up, nothing but walls, and thick ones too;
No sound shall tempt me agen, remember I
Have forswore books.

SECOND SERVANT

If you should be call'd to take your oath?

JUSTICE

I will forswear all oaths, rather than see
A thing but in the likeness of a book:
And I were condemn'd, I'll rather chuse to hang,
Than read agen; come in, and search all places,
They may be about the house, were the doors lock'd?

FIRST SERVANT

But the keys in 'em, and if they be gone,
They could not want wit to lock us in, Sir.

JUSTICE
Never was a man so miserably undone,
I would lose a limb, to see their rogueships totter.

[Exeunt.

[Enter **LADY** and **NURSE**.

LADY
Thy brothers daughter, saist, and born in Wales?

NURSE
I have long time desired to see her, and I hope
Your Ladyship will not be offended.

LADY
No, no.

NURSE
I should be happy, if she might be serviceable
To you Madam.

LADY
Beshrew me, but at first, she took me much,
Is she not like Maria? setting aside
Her language very like her, and I love her
The better for't, I prethee call her hither,
She speaks feat English.

NURSE
Why Guennith, Guennith, du hummah Guennith.
She is course Madam, after her countrey guise,
And were she in fine cloths—

LADY
I'll have her handsome:

[Enter **MARIA**.

What part of Wales were you born in?

MARIA
In Abehundis Mada ms .

NURSE
She speaks that name in Welsh, which we call Brecknock.

LADY
What can you do?

MARIA
Her was toe many tings in Walls, know not the fashion in Londons; her was milk the Cows, make seeze and butters, and spin very well the Welsh freeze, her was Cooke to te Mountain Cots, and sing very fine prittish tunes, was mage good ales and breds, and her know to dance on Sundays, marge you now Madams.

LADY
A pretty innocence, I do like her infinitely, Nurse,
And if I live—

[Enter **SERVANT**.

SERVANT
Here is Mr. Heartlove, Madam, come to see you.

LADY
Alas poor Gentleman, prethee admit him.

[Enter **HEARTLOVE** and **GENTLEMEN**.

HEARTLOVE
Madam, I am come to take my last leave.

LADY
How Sir?

HEARTLOVE
Of all my home affections, and my friends,
For the interest you had once in Maria,
I would acquaint you when I leave the kingdom.

LADY
Would there were any thing in my poor power
That might divert your Will, and make you happy,
I am sure I have wrong'd her too, but let your pardon
Assure me you are charitable; she's dead
Which makes us both sad: What do you look on?

FIRST GENTLEMEN
The likest face—

MARIA
Plesse us awle, why does that sentilman make such unders
and mazements at her, I know her not.

HEARTLOVE
Be not offended maid.

LADY
How the wench blushes, she represents Marias loss to him.

MARIA
Will the sentilman hurt her? pray you be her defences, was have mad phisnomies, is her troubled with Lunaticks in her prain pans, bless us awle.

HEARTLOVE
Where had you this face?

MARIA
Her faces be our none, I warrant her.

HEARTLOVE
I wonot hurt you, all the lineaments
That built Maria up; all those springing beauties
Dwell on this thing, change but her tongue I know her:
Let me see your hand.

MARIA
Du Guin. was never thieves, and robberies; here is no sindge in her hands warrant her.

HEARTLOVE
Trust me, the self-same white,
And softness, prethee speak our English Dialect.

MARIA
Ha leggs? what does her speage hard urds to her, to make poor Guenith ridicles, was no mannerly sentilman to abuse her.

HEARTLOVE
By the love,
That everlasting love I bear Maria—

MARIA
Maria, her name was Guenith, and good names, was poor else, oman maid, her have no fine kanags to madge her tricksie , yet in her own cuntries was held a fine ense her can tels her, and honest ense too, marg you dat now, her can keep her little legs close enough, warrant her.

LADY
How prettily this anger shews.

FIRST GENTLEMEN
She gabbles innocently.

HEARTLOVE
Madam farewel, and all good fortune dwell we'e,
With me my own affections; farewel Maid,
Fair gentle maid.

SECOND GENTLEMEN
She sighs.

MARIA
Du cat a whee.

HEARTLOVE
I cannot goe, there's somewhat calls me back.

MARIA
Poor Frank,
How gladly would I entertain thy love,
And meet thy worthy flame, but shame forbids me:
If please her Ladyship s dwell here with Guenith, and learn to spinn and card ull, to mage flannells, and linseyes ulseis, fall tawgco'd urds to her Ladyships urships for her.
The tears flow from him.
The tears of true affection, woe is me,
Oh cursed love that glories in maids miseries,
And true mens broken hearts.

LADY
Alas I pity him, the wench is rude, and knows you not, forgive her.

MARIA
Wy n e your nyes p ray you, though was porn in Walls 'mong craggy rocks, and mountains, yet heart is soft, look you hur can weep too, when hur see men mage prinie tears and lamentations.

HEARTLOVE
How hard she holds me!
Just as Maria did, weeps the same drops,
Now as I have a living soul, her si gh too;
What shall I think, is not your name Maria,
If it be not, delude me with so much charity
To say it is.

MARIA
Upon her life, you was mighty deal in love with some podies, your pale seekes and hollow nyes, and pantings upon her posom, know very well, because look you, her think her honest sentilman, you sall call her Maria.

HEARTLOVE
Good Madam, think not ill I am thus saucy.

LADY
Oh no Sir, be you not angry with the wench.

HEARTLOVE
I am most pleas'd.

FIRST GENTLEMEN
Lets interrupt him, he'll be mad outright else.

SECOND GENTLEMEN
Observe a little more.

HEARTLOVE
Would I could in your language beg a kiss.

MARIA
If her have necessities of a kiss, look you, dere is one in sarities.

HEARTLOVE
Let me suffer death,
If in my apprehension two twinn'd cherries
Be more a kinn, than her lips to Maria's:
And if this harsh illusion would but leave her,
She were the same, good Madam, shall I have
Your consent now?

LADY
To what?

HEARTLOVE
To give this Virgin to me.

LADY
She's not mine, this is her kinswoman,
And has more power to dispose; alas, I pity him.
Pray gentlem e n prevail with him to goe;
More that I wish his comfort than his absence.

HEARTLOVE
You have been always kind to me, will you
Deny me your fair Cosin?

NURSE
'Twere fit you first obtain'd her own consent.

HEARTLOVE
He is no friend that wishes my departure,
I doe not trouble you.

FIRST GENTLEMEN
'Tis not Maria.

HEARTLOVE
Her shadow is enough, I'll dwell with that,
Pursue your own ways, shall we live together?

MARIA
If her will come to morrow and tauge to her, her will tell her more of her meanings, and then if her be melancholy, her will sing her a Welch Song too, to make her merries, but Guenith was very honest; her was never love but one sentleman, and he was bear her great teal of good-ills too, was marry one day S. Davy, her give her five pair of white gloves, if her will dance at her weddings.

HEARTLOVE
All I am worth,
And all my hopes this strange voice would forsake her,
For then she shud be—prethee stay a little,
Hark in thine ear, dissemble not, but tell me,
And save my life; I know you are Maria:
Speak but as I doe, ten words to confirm me;
You have an English soul, do not disguise it
From me with these strange accents—She pinch'd hard
Again, and sigh'd.

LADY
What ails the Wench?

[Exit.

NURSE
Why, Guenith.

HEARTLOVE
She's gone too.

SECOND GENTLEMEN
Come leave this dream.

HEARTLOVE
A dream? I think so;
But 'twas a pleasing one, now I'll obey,
And forget all these wonders, lead the way.

[Exeunt.

ACTUS QUARTUS

SCÆNA PRIMA

Enter **WILD-BRAIN** and **TOBIE.**

WILD-BRAIN
Honest Toby?

TOBIE
Sweet Mr. Wild-Brain,—I am glad I ha met w'ye.

WILD-BRAIN
Why, did my Aunt send for me?

TOBIE
Your Aunt's a mortal, and thinks not on you
For ought I can perceive.

WILD-BRAIN
Is my cosin alive agen?

TOBIE
Neither, and yet we do not hear
That she's buried.

WILD-BRAIN
What should make thee glad then?

TOBIE
What should make me glad? have I not cause,
To see your Princely body well, and walk thus,
Look blithe and bonny, and your Wardrobe whole still?

WILD-BRAIN
The case is clear, and I ha found a Mine,
A perfect Indie, since my Aunt cashier'd me;
What think'st of this?

TOBIE
Oh delicate bells.

WILD-BRAIN
Thou puttest me in mind,
We are to ring anon, I mean t to send for thee;
Meet me at the old Parish Church.

TOBIE

Say no more.

WILD-BRAIN
When thy Lady is a bed, we ha conspir'd
A midnight peal for joy.

TOBIE
If I fail, hang me i' th' bell-ropes.

WILD-BRAIN
And how? and how does my Aunt?

TOBIE
She's up to th' ears in Law;
I do so whirl her to the Counsellors chambers,
And back again, and bounce her for more money,
And too again, I know not what they do with her;
But she's the merriest thing among these Law-drivers;
And in their studies half a day together;
If they do get her with Magna Charta, she swears,
By all the ability of her old body,
She will so claw the Justice, she will sell
The tiles of the house she vows, and Sack out o'th' Cellar,
(That she worships to Idolatry) but she'll hang him.

WILD-BRAIN
I would she could: but hark thee honest Toby.
If a man have a Mistriss, may we not,
Without my Aunt's leave, borrow now and then
A Coach to tumble in, towards the Exchange,
And so forth?

TOBIE
A Mistriss?

WILD-BRAIN
She may be thine when we are married.

TOBIE
Command, I'll carry you both in pomp;
And let my Lady go a foot a Law-catching,
And exercise her corns: where is she Master John?

WILD-BRAIN
'Shat see her.

TOBIE
Shall we ring for her?

WILD-BRAIN
And drink her health?

TOBIE
Drink stifly for five hours.

WILD-BRAIN
We'll drink fifteen.

TOBIE
Tonight? we will ha twenty Torches then,
And through the streets drive on triumphantly;
Triumphantly we'll drive, by my Lad y es door,
As I am a Christian Coachman, I will rattle you
And Urine in her porch, and she shall fear me:
If you say more, I shall run mad outright,
I will drink Sack, and surfeit instantly;
I know not where I am now.

[Exit.

[Enter **LURCHER**.

WILD-LOVE
Hold for thy buttons sake, the knave's transported.

LURCHER
Jack Wild-Brain?

WILD-BRAIN
Honest Tom, how thrives the fellonious world with thee now?

LURCHER
You look and talk as you were much exalted.

WILD-BRAIN
Th'art i'th' right Tom. I'll tell thee first,
I ha shook off my Aunt, and yet I live still,
And drink, and sing; her house had like to ha spoil'd me;
I keep no hours now;
Nor need any false key
To the old womans Cabinets, I ha money
Upon my word, and pawn no oaths to th' Butler.
No matrimonial protestations
For Sack-possets to the Chambermaid,
I praise my Fate, there be more ways to th' wood Tom.

LURCHER
Prethee release my wonder.

WILD-BRAIN
I'll increase it, wipe thine eyes,
Here is a chain worth money, and some man had it,
A foolis h Diamond, and other trifles—

LURCHER
The very same, Oh Gipsey! Infidel!
All that I sweat, and ventur'd my neck for,
He has got already; who would trust a strumpet:

WILD-BRAIN
This? This is nothing to what I possess
At home.

LURCHER
What home?

WILD-BRAIN
A house that shall be nameless;
The Mistriss of it mine too, such a piece
For flesh and blood, added to that so loving—

LURCHER
Is she married?

WILD-BRAIN
I know not, nor I care not;
But such a prize, so mounting, so delicious,
Thou wilt run mad, I'll tell thee more hereafter.

LURCHER
Nay, prethee a word more.

WILD-BRAIN
I took no pains to find out all this Paradise,
My destiny threw me upon't i'th dark, I found it
Wanting a Lodging too.

LURCHER
No old acquaintance?

WILD-BRAIN
Never, never saw her;
But these things happen not in every age:
I cannot stay, if thou wilt meet anon

At my own randevow, thou knowest the Tavern,
We'll sup together, after that a company
Of merry lads have made a match to ring.

LURCHER
You keep your exercise, i'th' old Church?

WILD-BRAIN
No other,
There is no Musick to the Bells, we wo'd
Have Bonfires if we durst, and thou wo'd come
It shall cost thee nothing Tom, hang pilfering,
And keep me company, in time I may
Shew thee my wench too.

LURCHER
I cannot promise; but you will be there?

WILD-BRAIN
We'll toss the Bells, and make the Steeple
Roar boy, but come to supper then.

LURCHER
My hand, and expect me:
Yes, I will come or send, and to some purpose;
Art come boy?

[Enter **BOY** with Gown, Beard, and Constables staff.

Excellent, Knave, how didst thou purchase these?

BOY
The staff I stole last night from a sleeping Constable;
The rest I borrowed by my acquaintance with
The Players boyes; you were best to lose no time, Sir.

LURCHER
So, so, help boy, 'tis very well, do I not look
Like one that breaks the Kings peace with authority?
You know your charge, prepare things handsomely,
My diligent boy, and leave me to my office.

BOY
There wants nothing already; but I fly Sir.

[Exit.

LURCHER

Now Fortune prove no slut, and I'll adore thee.

SERVANT [Within]
Whose there?

[Knocks.

LURCHER
A friend wo'd speak with Master Justice.

SERVANT
Who are you?

LURCHER
I am the Constable.

SERVANT
My Master is not at leasure to hear business.

LURCHER
How? Not at leasure to do the King service;
Take heed what you say, Sir; I know his worship,
If he kn e w my business, would no excuse.

SERVANT
You must go to another Justice, I'll assure
My Master is not well in health.

LURCHER
I know not,
But if your worshipful be not at leasure
To do himself a benefit, I am gone Sir,
An infinite benefit, and the State shall thank him for't;
Thank him, and think on him too; I am an Officer.
And know my place, but I do love the Justice;
I honor any authority above me:
Beside, he is my neighbor, and I worship him.

SERVANT
You have no Books, nor Ballads, Mr Constable,
About you?

LURCHER
What should I doe with Books? does it become
A man of my place to understand such matters?
Pray call your Master, if he please to follow me,
I shall discover to him such a plot,
Shall get him everlasting fame, I'll be hang'd for't,

And he be not knighted instantly, and for reward
Have some of the malefactors Lands, I'll bring him too;
But I cannot dally time.

JUSTICE [Within]
Who's that?

SERVANT
A Constable Sir, would speak about some business,
He says will bring you Fame, and mighty profit.

LURCHER
Please your worship come down, I'll make you happy;
The notabl'st piece of villany I have in hand Sir,
And you shall find it out; I ha made choice
To bring your worship to the first knowledge, and
Thank me, as you find the good on't afterwards.

JUSTICE
What is it? Treason?

LURCHER
'Tis little better, I can tell you I have lodg'd
A crew of the most rank and desperate villains:
They talk of robberies and waies they did 'em;
And how they left men bound i n their studies.

JUSTICE
With Books and Ballads?

LURCHER
That Sir, that, and murders,
And thousand knaveries more, they're very rich Sir,
In Money, Jewels, Chains, and a hundred more
Devices.

JUSTICE
Happy, happy Constable, I meet ye
At the back door, get ready knaves.

LURCHER
Not a man I beseech you,
I have privately appointed strength about me,
They cannot start, your men would breed suspition;
All my desire is, you would come alone;
That you might have the hope of the enterprise,
That you might hear 'em first, and then proceed, Sir.

JUSTICE
I come, I come.

LURCHER
'Tis very well.

[Exit.

JUSTICE
Keep all my doors fast, 'tis something late.

LURCHER
So, so, and please your worship Ile direct you.

[Enter **BOY**.

BOY
My Master staies, I doubt his lime-twigs catch not,
If they doe, all's provided; but I all
This while forget my own state, fair Maria
Is certainly alive, I met her in
Another habit, with her Nurse, 'twas she:
There is some trick in't, but when this is over,
I'll find it out, this project for the Usurer
May have good effect; however, 'twill be sport
To mortifie him a little;

[Enter **LURCHER**.

He's come without him:
Have you fail'd, Sir?

LURCHER
Prosper'd? my little Ingineer; away,
He is i'th' next room, be not you seen, sirrah.

[Exit.

BOY
The pitfall's ready, never Justice
Was catcht in such a nooze: e'er he get out,
He shall run through a scouring purgatory,
Shall purge him to the quick, 'tis night already.

[Exit.

[Enter **ALGRIPE** and **LURCHER**.

LURCHER
Come softly, yet Sir, softly, are you not weary?

JUSTICE
Th'ast brought me into a melancholy place,
I see no creature.

LURCHER
This is, Sir, their Den
Where they suppose themselves secure, I am faint,
With making haste; but I must be thus troubled,
And therefore never go without a
Cordial; Seems to drink.
Without this I should dye;
How it refreshes me
Already! will't please your worship? I might have had
The manners to ha' let you drink before me;
Now am I lusty.

JUSTICE
'T has a good taste.

LURCHER
Taste? how d'ye find the virtue, nay Sir, spare it not:
My wife has the Receipt, does it not stir
Your Worships body? when you come to examine,
'Twill make you speak like thunder.

JUSTICE
Hoy he.

LURCHER
It works already.

JUSTICE
Is there never a chair, I was wearier than I thought,
But who shall we have to take 'em. Mr. Constable?

LURCHER
Let me alone, when I but give the watch-word
We will have men enough to surprize an Army.

JUSTICE
I begin to be sleepy; what, hast a chair?

[Enter **ANOTHER** with a chair.

LURCHER

They do not dream of us, 'tis early rising;
Care, care, and early rising, Common-wealths men
Are ever subject to the nods; sit down, Sir,
A short nap is not much amiss; so, so, he's fast;
Fast as a fish i'th' net, he has winking powder
Shall work upon him to our wish, remove him,
Nay, we may cut him into collops now
And he ne'r feel; have you prepar'd the vault, sirrah?

BOY
Yes, yes, Sir, every thing in's place.

LURCHER
When we have plac'd him, you and I boy
Must about another project hard by, his potion
Will bind him sure enough till we return,
This villany weighs mainly, But we'll purge ye.

[Exit.

[Bells ring.

[Enter **SEXTON**.

SEXTON
Now for mine ears, mine ears be constant to me;
They ring a wager, and I must deal justly, ha boys.

[Enter **LURCHER** and **BOY.**

LURCHER
Dost hear 'em, hark, these be the Ringers?

BOY
Are you sure the same?

LURCHER
Or my directions fail;
The coast is clear:
How the bells go! how daintily they tumble!
And methinks they seem to say; Fine fools I'll fit you.

SEXTON
Excellent agen, good boys—oh that was nought.

LURCHER
Who's that?

BOY
Be you conceal'd by any means yet, hark,
They stop, I hope they'll to't agen, close Sir.

[Enter **WILD-BRAIN, TOBIE, RINGERS.**

WILD-BRAIN
A palpable knock.

RINGERS
'Twas none.

TOBIE
Be judg'd by the Sexton then,
If I have ears.

SEXTON
A knock, a knock, a gross one.

TOBIE
Carman, your gallon of wine, you ring most impiously,
Art thou o'th' worshipful company of the Knights o'th West,
And handle a bell with no more dexterity?
You think you are in Thames-street
Justling the Carts: oh a clean hand's a Jewel.

BOY
Good speed to your good exercise.

TOBIE
Y' are welcome.

BOY
I come, Sir, from a Gentleman, and neighbor hard by,
One that loves your Musick well.

TOBIE
He may have more on't,
Handle a bell, as you were haling timber;
Gross, gross, and base, absurd.

RINGERS
I'll mend it next peal.

BOY
To intreat a knowledge of you, whether it be
By the Ear you ring thus cunningly, or by the Eye;
For to be plain, he has laid ten pounds upon't.

WILD-BRAIN
But which way has he laid?

BOY
That your Ear guides you,
And not your Eye.

TOBIE
Has won, has won, the Ear's our only instrument:

BOY
But how shall we be sure on't.

TOBIE
Put all the lights out, to what end serve our eyes then?

WILD-BRAIN
A plain Case.

BOY
You say true, 'tis a fine cunning thing to ring by th' Ear sure:
And can you ring i' th' dark so?

WILD-BRAIN
All night long, boy.

BOY
'Tis wonderful, let this be certain Gentlemen,
And half his wager he allows among ye;
Is't possible you should ring so?

TOBIE
Possible, thou art a child, I'll ring when I am dead drunk
Out with the lights, no twinkling of a candle,
I know my rope too, as I know my nose,
And can bang it soundly i'th' dark, I warrant you.

WILD-LOVE
Come, let's confirm him straight, and win the wager.

[Exit.

BOY
Let me hear to strengthen me;
And when y'ave rung, I'll bring the money to you.

LURCHER

So, so, follow 'em;
They shall have a cool reward, one hath gold of mine,
Good store in's pocket,—

[Ring.

But this will be reveng'd in a short warning.
They are at it lustily; hey, how wantonly
They ring away their cloaths, how it delights me.

BOY
Here, here, Sir.

[Enter **BOY** with cloaths.

LURCHER
Hast Wild-Brain's?

BOY
His whole case, Sir; I felt it out, and by the guards
This should be the Coachmans, another suit too.

LURCHER
Away boy, quickly now to the Usurer,
His hour to wake approaches.

BOY
That once finished,
You'll give me leave to play, Sir: here they come.

[Exit.

[Enter **WILD-BRAIN, TOBIE**, and **RINGERS**.

WILD-BRAIN
I am monstrous weary.

TOBIE
Fie, how I sweat! Reach me my cloak to cover me,
I run to oyl like a Porpise; 'twas a brave peal.

SEXTON
Let me light my candle first, then I'll wait on you.

WILD-BRAIN
A very brave peal.

TOBIE

Carman, you came in close now.

WILD-BRAIN
Sure 'tis past midnight.

RINGERS
No stirring in the streets I hear.

TOBIE
Walk further, was that a pillar? 'tis harder than my nose,
Where's the boy promis'd us five pounds?

WILD-BRAIN
Room, I sweat still; come, come, my cloak,
I shall take cold.

[Enter **SEXTON**.

SEXTON
Where lies it?

WILD-BRAIN
Here, here, and all our cloaths.

SEXTON
Where, where?

RINGERS
I'th' corner.

TOBIE
Is thy candle blind too, give me the bottle,
I can drink like a Fish now, like an Elephant.

SEXTON
Here are the corners, but here are no cloaths;
Yes, here is a cuff.

WILD-BRAIN
A cuff? give me the candle,
Cuffes wonot cover me—I smell the knavery.

TOBIE
Is't come to a cuff? my whole suit turned to a button?

WILD-BRAIN
Now am I as cold again as though 'twere Christmas;
Cold with my fear, I'll never ring by the ear more.

TOBIE
My new cloaths vanish'd?

WILD-BRAIN
All my cloaths Toby.

RINGERS
Here's none.

TOBIE
Not one of my dragons wings left to adorn me,
Have I muted all my feathers?

WILD-BRAIN
Cheated by the ear; a plot to put out the candle;
I could be mad; my chain, my rings, the gold, the gold.

TOBIE
The cold, the cold I cry, and I cry truly,
Not one sleeve, nor a cape of a cloak to warm me.

WILD-BRAIN
What miserable fools were we!

TOBIE
We had e'en best, gentlemen,
Every man chuse his rope again, and fasten it,
And take a short turn to a better fortune,
To be bawds to our miseries, and put our own lights out!

WILD-BRAIN
Prethee Sexton lets have a fire at thy house.
A good fire, we'll pay thee some way for't, I am stone cold.

SEXTON
Alas I pity you, come quickly Gentlemen.

WILD-BRAIN
Sure I ha been in a dream, I had no Mistriss,
Nor gold, nor cloaths, but am a ringing rascal.

TOBIE
Fellows in affliction, let's take hands all,
Now are we fit for tumblers.

[Enter **LURCHER** and **OTHERS,** bringing in **ALGRIPE.**

LURCHER
So, so, presently his sleep will leave him.
And wonder seize upon him,
Bid 'em within be ready.

JUSTICE
What sound's this?
What horrid dinne? what dismal place is this?
I never saw before, and now behold it;
But by the half light of a Lamp, that burns here:
My spirits shake, tremble through my body;
Help, help,

[Enter **TWO FURIES**, with black Tapers.

Mercy protect me, my soul quakes,
What dreadful apparitions! how I shudder!

FIRST & SECOND FURIES
Algripe.

JUSTICE
What are you?

FIRST FURY
We are hellhounds, hellhounds, that have commission
From the Prince of darkness,
To fetch thy black soul to him.

JUSTICE
Am I not alive still?

FIRST FURY
Thou art, but we have brought thee instruments
Will quickly rid thy miserable life, Stabb.

SECOND FURY
Poyson.

FIRST FURY
Hang thy self, this choice is offer'd.

SECOND FURY
Thou canst not hope for heaven; thy base soul is
Lost to all hope of mercy.

FIRST FURY
Quickly, quickly,

The torments cool.

SECOND FURY
And all the Fiends expect thee.
Come with us to that pit of endless horror,
Or we will force thee.

JUSTICE
Oh, oh, oh.

FIRST FURY
Groans are too late, sooner the ravisher,
Whose soul is hurl'd into eternal frost,
Stung with the force of twenty thousand winters,
To punish the distempers of his blood,
Shall hope to get from thence, than thou avoid
The certainty of meeting hell where he is.
Shall murderers be there for ever dying,
Their souls shot through with Adders, torn on Engines,
Dying as many deaths for killing one,
Could any imagination number them,
As there be moments in eternity:
And shall that Justice spare thee, that hast slain,
Murdered by thy extortion so many?

JUSTICE
Oh, oh.

SECOND FURY
Do execution quickly, or we'll carry thee alive to hell.

JUSTICE
Gently, gentle devils, do not force me
To kill my self, nor do not you do't for me;
Oh let me live, I'll make amends for all.

FIRST FURY
Tell us of thy repentance? perjur'd villain,
Pinch off his flesh, he must be whipt, salted and whipt.

JUSTICE
Oh misery of miseries!

BOTH FURIES
Tear his accursed limbs, to hell with him, ha!
A mischief on that innocent face, away.

[Enter **BOY** like an Angel, creeps in.

BOY
Malicious furies hence, choak not the seeds
Of holy penitence.

JUSTICE
This must be an Angel,
How at his presence the fiends crawl away!
Here is some light of mercy.

BOY
Be thou wise,
And entertain it, wretched, wretched man;
What poor defence hath all thy wealth been to thee?
What says thy conscience now?

JUSTICE
Be my good Angel, here I promise thee,
To become honest, and renounce all villany;
Enjoyn me any pennance, I'll build Churches;
A whole City of Hospitals.

BOY
Take heed,
There is no dallying, nor are these impos'd.

JUSTICE
Name any thing within my power, sweet Angel;
And if I do not faithfully perform it,
Then whip me every day, burn me each minute,
Whole years together let me freeze to Isicles.

BOY
I'th' number of thy foul oppressions;
Thou hast undone a faithful Gentleman,
By taking forfeit of his Land.

JUSTICE
Young Lurcher,
I do confess.

BOY
He lives most miserable,
And in despair may hang or drown himself;
Prevent his ruine, or his blood will be
More sin in thy account: hast thou forgotten
He had a sister?

JUSTICE
I do well remember it.

BOY
Couldst thou for Mammon break thy solemn vow,
Made once to that unhappy maid, that weeps
A thousand tears a day for thy unkindness,
Was not thy faith contracted, and thy heart?
And couldst thou marry another?

JUSTICE
But she is dead,
And I will make true satisfaction.

BOY
What do I instance these that hast been false
To all the world.

JUSTICE
I know it, and will henceforth
Practice repentance, do not frown sweet Angel;
I will restore all Mortgages, forswear
Abominable Usury, live chaste;
For I have been wanton in my shroud, my age;
And if that poor innocent maid, I so abus'd,
Be living, I will marry her, and spend
My days to come religiously.

BOY
I was commanded but a Messenger
To tell thee this, and rescue thee from those,
Whose malice would have dragg'd thee quick to hell,
If thou abuse this mercy and repent not,
Double damnation will expect thee for it;
But if thy life be virtuous hereafter,
A blessedness shall reward thy good example,
Thy fright hath much distracted thy weak sences,
Drink of this viol, and renew thy spirits
I ha done my office, think on't and be happy.

LURCHER
So, so, he gapes already, now he's fast;
Thou hast acted rarely, but this is not all;
First, help to convey him out o' th' vault.

BOY
You will dispense with me now, as you promis'd, Sir.

LURCHER
We will make shift without thee, th'ast done well,
By our device this bondage may scape hell.

[Exit.

[Enter **LADY, NURSE, MARIA.**

LADY
Didst think Maria, this poor outside, and
Dissembling of thy voice could hide thee from
A mothers searching eye, though too much fear,
Lest thou wert not the same, might blind a Lover
That thought thee dead too; oh my dear Maria,
I hardly kept my joyes in from betraying thee:
Welcome again to life, we shall find out
The mystery of thy absence; conceal
Thy person still, for Algripe must not know thee:
And exercise this pretty Dialect;
If there be any course in Law to free thee,
Thou shalt not be so miserable; be silent
Good Nurse.

NURSE
You shall not need to fear me, Madam,
I do not love the usuring Jew so well;
Beside, 'twas my trick to disguise her so.

LADY
Be not dejected Mall.

MARIA
Your care may comfort me;
But I despair of happiness:
Heartlove, I dare not see him.

NURSE
We'll withdraw.

LADY
I shall but grieve to see his passions too,
Since there's no possibility to relieve him.

[Enter **HEARTLOVE.**

HEARTLOVE
The world's a Labyrinth, where unguided men
Walk up and down to find their weariness;

No sooner have we measured with much toil
One crooked path with hope to gain our freedom,
But it betrays us to a new affliction;
What a strange mockery will man become
Shortly to all the creatures?
Oh Mariah!

If thou be'st dead, why does thy shadow fright me?
Sure 'tis because I live; were I but certain
To meet thee in one grave, and that our dust
Might have the priviledge to mix in silence,
How quickly should my soul shake off this burthen!

[Enter **BOY**.

BOY
Thus far my wishes have success, I'll lose
No time: Sir, are not you call'd Mr. Heartlove?
Pardon my rudeness.

HEARTLOVE
What does that concern
Thee Boy, 'tis a name cannot advantage thee;
And I am weary on't.

BOY
Had you conceal'd,
Or I forgot it, Sir, so large were my
Directions, that you could not speak this language,
But I should know you by your sorrow.

HEARTLOVE
Thou
Wert well inform'd, it seems; well, what's your business?

BOY
I come to bring you comfort.

HEARTLOVE
Is Maria
Alive agen? that's somewhat, and yet not
Enough to make my expectation rise, to
Past half a blessing; since we cannot meet
To make it up a full one; th'art mistaken.

BOY
When you have heard me, you'll think otherwise:
In vain I should report Maria living:

The comfort that I bring you, must depend
Upon her death.

HEARTLOVE
Th'art a dissembling boy,
Some one has sent thee to mock me; though my anger
Stoop not to punish thy green years unripe
For malice; did I know what person sent thee
To tempt my sorrow thus, I should reveng it.

BOY
Indeed I have no thought so uncharitable,
Nor am I sent to grieve you, let me suffer
More punishment than ever boy deserv'd,
If you do find me false; I serve a Mistriss
Would rather dye than play with your misfortunes;
Then good Sir hear me out.

HEARTLOVE
Who is your Mistriss?

BOY
Before I name her, give me some encouragement,
That you receive her message: she is one
That is full acquainted with your misery,
And can bring such a portion of her sorrow
In every circumstance so like your own,
You'll love and pity her, and wish your griefs
Might marry one anothers.

HEARTLOVE
Thou art wild.
Canst thou bring comfort from so sad a creature?
Her miserable story can at best,
But swell my Volume, large enough already.

BOY
She was late belov'd, as you were, promis'd faith
And marriage; and was worthy of a better
Than he, that stole Maria's heart.

HEARTLOVE
How's that?

BOY
Just as Maria dealt with your affection,
Did he that married her deal with my Mistriss,
When careless both of Honor and Religion;

They cruelly gave away their hearts to strangers.

HEARTLOVE
Part of this truth I know, but prethee boy
Proceed to that thou cam'st for; thou didst Promise
Something, thy language cannot hitherto
Encourage me to hope for.

BOY
That I come to:
My Mistriss thus unkindly dealt withal,
You may imagine, wanted no affliction;
And had e'r this, wept her self dry as Marble,
Had not your fortune come to her relief,
And twinn to her own sorrow brought her comfort.

HEARTLOVE
Could the condition of my fate so equal,
Lessen her sufferings?

BOY
I know not how
Companions in grief sometimes diminish
And make the pressure easie by degrees:
She threw her troubles off, remembring yours,
And from her pity of your wrongs, there grew
Affection to your person thus increas'd,
And with it, confidence, that those whom Nature
Had made so even in their weight of sorrow,
Could not but love as equally one another,
Were things but well prepar'd, this gave her boldness
To employ me thus far.

HEARTLOVE
A strange message, boy.

BOY
If you incline to meet my Mistriss love,
It may beget your comforts; besides that,
'Tis some revenge, that you above their scorn
And pride can laugh at them, whose perjury
Hath made you happy, and undone themselves.

HEARTLOVE
Have you done boy?

BOY
Only this little more;

When you but see, and know my Mistriss well,
You will forgive my tediousness, she's fair,
Fair as Maria was.

HEARTLOVE
I'll hear no more,
Go foolish boy, a n d tell thy fonder Mistriss
She has no second Faith to give away;
And mine was given to Maria, though her death
Allow me freedom, see the Picture of her.

[Enter **MARIA, NURSE**.

I would give ten thousand Empires for the substance;
Yet for Maria's sake, whose divine Figure
That rude frame carries, I will love this counterfeit
Above all the world, and had thy Mistriss all
The grace and blossom of her sex; now she
Is gone, that was a walking Spring of beauty,
I would not look upon her.

BOY
Sir, your pardon,
I have but done a message, as becomes
A servant, nor did she on whose commands
I gladly waited, bid me urge her love
To your disquiet, she would chide my diligence
If I should make you angry.

HEARTLOVE
Pretty boy.

BOY
Indeed I fear I have offended you:
Pray if I have, enjoyn me any pennance for it:
I have perform'd one duty, and could as willingly
To purge my fault, and shew I suffer with you,
Plead your cause to another.

HEARTLOVE
And I'll take thee
At thy word boy, thou hast a moving language,
That pretty innocent, Copy of Maria
Is all I love, I know not how to speak,
Winn her to think well of me, and I will
Reward thee to thy wishes.

BOY

I undertake
Nothing for gain, but since you have resolv'd,
To love no other, I'll be faithful to you,
And my prophetick thoughts bid me already
Say I shall prosper.

HEARTLOVE
Thou wert sent to bless me.

BOY
Pray give us opportunity.

HEARTLOVE
Be happy.

[Exit.

NURSE
He's gone.

BOY
With your fair leave Mistriss.

MARIA
Have you pusinesse with her pray you

BOY
I have a message from a Gentleman,
Please you vouchsafe your ear more private.

NURSE
You shall have my absence Neece.

[Exit.

MARIA
Was the sentleman afear'd to declare his matters openly, here was no bodies was not very honest, if her like not her errands the petter, was wist to keep her preaths to cool her porridges, can tell her, that now for aule her private hearings and tawgings.

BOY
You may, if please you, find another language.
And with less pains be understood.

MARIA
What is her meaning?

BOY

Come, pray speak your own English.

MARIA

Have boyes lost her itts and memories? plesse us aule.

BOY

I must be plain then, come, I know you are
Maria, this thin vail cannot obscure you:
I'll tell the world you live, I have not lost ye,
Since first with grief and shame to be surpriz'd,
A violent trance took away shew of life;
I could discover by what accident
You were convey'd away at midnight, in
Your coffin, could declare the place, and minute,
When you reviv'd, and what you have done since as perfectly—

MARIA

Alas, I am betraid to new misfortunes.

BOY

You are not, for my knowledge, I'll be dumb
For ever, rather than be such a traitor;
Indeed I pity you, and bring no thoughts,
But full of peace, call home your modest blood,
Pale hath too long usurp'd upon your face;
Think upon love agen, and the possession
Of full blown joyes, now ready to salute you.

MARIA

These words undo me more than my own griefs.

BOY

I see how fear would play the tyrant with you,
But I'll remove suspition; have you in
Your heart, an entertainment for his love
To whom your Virgin faith made the first promise?

MARIA

If thou mean'st Heartlove, thou dost wound me still,
I have no life without his memory,
Nor with it any hope to keep it long:
Thou seest I walk in darkness like a thief,
That fears to see the world in his own shape,
My very shadow frights me, 'tis a death
To live thus, and not look day in the face,
Away, I know thee not.

BOY

You shall hereafter know, and thank me Lady,
I'll bring you a discharge at my next visit,
Of all your fears, be content, fair Maria,
'Tis worth your wonder.

MARIA
Impossible.

BOY
Be wise and silent,
Dress your self, you shall be what you wish.

MARIA
Do this, and be
My better Angel.

BOY
All your care's on me.

[Exeunt.

ACTUS QUINTUS

SCÆNA PRIMA

Enter **LURCHER**, and **BOY**.

LURCHER
I must applaud thy diligence.

BOY
It had been nothing
To have left him in the Porch; I call'd his servants,
With wonders they acknowledg'd him, I pretended
It was some spice sure of the falling sickness,
And that, 'twas charity to bring him home;
They rubb'd and chaf'd him, ply'd him with Strong water,
Still he was senseless, clamors could not wake him;
I wish'd 'em then get him to bed, they did so,
And almost smother'd him with ruggs and pillows;
And 'cause they should have no cause to suspect me,
I watch'd them till he wak'd.

LURCHER
'Twas excellent.

BOY

When his time came to yawn, and stretch himself,
I bid 'em not be hasty to discover
How he was brought home; his eyes fully open
With trembling he began to call his servants,
And told 'em he had seen strange visions,
That should convert him from his heathen courses;
They wondred, and were silent, there he preach'd
How sweet the air of a contented conscience
Smelt in his nose now, ask'd 'em all forgiveness
For their hard pasture since they liv'd with him;
Bid 'em believe, and fetch out the cold Sur-loin;
Pierce the strong beer, and let the neighbors joy in't:
The conceal'd Muskadine should now lie open
To every mouth; that he would give to th' poor,
And mend their wages; that his doors should be
Open to every miserable sutor.

LURCHER

What said his servants then?

BOY

They durst not speak,
But blest themselves, and the strange means that had
Made him a Christian in this over-joy,
I took my leave, and bad 'em say their prayers,
And humor him, lest he turn'd Jew agen.

LURCHER

Enough, enough. Who's this?

[Enter **TOBIE**.

'Tis one of my ringers; stand close, my Ladies Coachman.

TOBIE

Buy a mat for a bed, buy a mat;
Would I were at rack and manger among my horses;
We have divided the Sextons
Houshold-stuff among us, one has the rugg, and he's
Turn'd Irish, and another has a blanket, and he must beg in't,
The sheets serve another for a frock, and with the bed-cord,
He may pass for a Porter, nothing but the mat would fall
To my share, which with the help of a tune and a hassock
Out o'th' Church, may disguise me till I get home;
A pox o' bell-ringing by the ear, if any man take me
At it agen, let him pull mine to the Pillory: I could wish
I had lost mine ears, so I had my cloaths again:

The weather wo'not allow this fashion,
I do look for an Ague besides.

LURCHER
How the raskal shakes!

TOBIE
Here are company:
Buy a Mat for a Bed, buy a Mat,
A hassock for your feet, or a Piss clean and sweet;
Buy a Mat for a Bed, buy a Mat:
Ringing I renounce thee, I'll never come to church more.

LURCHER
You with a Mat.

TOBIE
I am call'd.
If any one should offer to buy my Mat, what a case were I in?
Oh that I were in my Oat-tub with a horse-loaf,
Something to hearten me:
I dare not hear 'em;
Buy a mat for a bed, buy a mat.

LURCHER
He's deaf.

TOBIE
I am glad I am: buy a mat for a bed.

LURCHER
How the raskal sweats! What a pickle he's in!
Every street he goes through will be a new torment.

TOBIE
If ever I meet at midnight more a jangling:
I am cold, and yet I drop; buy a mat for a bed, buy a mat.

LURCHER
He has punishment enough.

[Exit.

[Enter **WILD-BRAIN**.

Who's this, my tother youth? he is turn'd Bear.

WILD-BRAIN

I am halfe afraid of my self: this poor shift
I got 'o th' Sexton to convey me handsomly
To some harbor, the wench will hardly know me;
They'll take me for some Watchman o'th' parish;
I ha ne'r a penny left me, that's one comfort;
And ringing has begot a monstrous stomach,
And that's another mischief: I were best go home,
For every thing will scorn me in this habit.
Besides, I am so full of these young bell-ringers;
If I get in adoors, not the power o'th' countrey,
Nor all my Aunts curses shall disembogue me.

LURCHER
Bid her come hither presently,—hum, 'tis he.

[Exit. **SERVANT.**

WILD-BRAIN
I am betraid to one that will eternally laugh at me,
Three of these rogues will jeer a horse to death.

LURCHER
'Tis Mr. Wild-Brain sure, and yet me thinks
His fashion's strangely alt'red, sirrah Watchman,
You ragamuffin, turn you louzie Bears skin:
You with the Bed-rid Bill.

WILD-BRAIN
H'as found me out;
There's no avoiding him, I had rather now
Be arraign'd at Newgate for a robbery,
Than answer to his Articles: your Will Sir,
I am in haste.

LURCHER
Nay, then I will make bold wi'ye;
A Watchman, and asham'd to shew his countenance,
His face of authority? I have seen that physiognomy;
Were you never in prison for pilfering?

WILD-BRAIN
How the rogue worries me.

LURCHER
Why may not this
Be the villain robb'd my house last night,
And walks disguis'd in this malignant rugg,
Arm'd with a tun of Iron? I will have you

Before a Magistrate.

WILD-BRAIN
What will become of me?

LURCHER
What art thou? speak.

WILD-BRAIN
I am the wandring Jew, and please your worship.

LURCHER
By your leave Rabbi, I will shew you then
A Synagogue, iclip't Bridewel, where you,
Under correction, may rest your self:
You have brought a bill to guard you, there be dog-whips
To firk such rugg'd currs, whips without bells
Indeed.

WILD-BRAIN
Bells.

LURCHER
How he sweats!

WILD-BRAIN
I must be known, as good at first; now jeer on,
But do not anger me too impudently,
The Rabbi will be mov'd then.

LURCHER
How? Jack Wild-Brain,
What time o'th' Moon man, ha? what strange bells
Hast in thy brains?

WILD-BRAIN
No more bells,
No more bells, they ring backwards.

LURCHER
Why, where's the wench, the blessing that befel thee?
The unexpected happiness? where's that Jack?
Where are thy golden days?

WILD-BRAIN
It was his trick, as sure as I am louzie,
But how to be reveng'd—

LURCHER

Fie, fie, Jack,
Marry a Watchmans widow in thy young daies,
With a revenue of old Iron and a Rugg?
Is this the Paragon, the dainty piece,
The delicate divine rogue?

WILD-BRAIN

'Tis enough, I am undone,
Mark'd for a misery, and so leave prating;
Give me my Bill.

LURCHER

You need not ask your Taylors,
Unless you had better Linings; it may be,
To avoid suspition, you are going thus
Disguis'd to your fair Mistriss.

WILD-BRAIN

Mock no further,
Or as I live, I'll lay my Bill o' thy pate,
I'll take a Watchmans fury into my fingers,
To ha no judgement to distinguish persons,
And knock thee down.

LURCHER

Come, I ha done, and now
Will speak some comfort to thee, I will lead thee
Now to my Mistriss hitherto conceal'd;
She shall take pity on thee too, she loves
A handsome man; thy misery invites me
To do thee good, I'll not be jealous, Jack;
Her beauty shall commend it self; but do not,
When I have brought you into grace, supplant me.

WILD-BRAIN

Art thou in earnest? by this cold Iron—

LURCHER

No oaths, I am not costive; here she comes.

[Enter **MISTRISS**.

Sweet-heart, I have brought a Gentleman,
A friend of mine to be acquainted with you,
He's other than he seems; why d'ye stare thus?

MISTRISS

Oh Sir, forgive me, I have done ye wrong.

LURCHER
What's the matter? didst ever see her afore Jack?

WILD-BRAIN
Prethee do what thou wot wi'me, if thou hast
A mind, hang me up quickly.

LURCHER
Never despair, I'll give thee my share rather,
Take her, I hope she loves thee at first sight,
She has petticoats will patch thee up a suit;
I resign all, only I'll keep these trifles.
I took some pains for 'em, I take it Jack;
What think you pink of beauty, come let me
Counsel you both to marry, she has a trade,
If you have audacity to hook in Gamesters:
Let's ha a wedding, you will be wondrous rich;
For she is impudent, and thou art miserable;
'Twill be a rare match.

MISTRISS
As you are a man, forgive me, I'll redeem all.

LURCHER
You wo'not to this geer of marriage then?

WILD-BRAIN
No, no, I thank you Tom, I can watch for
A groat a night, and be every gentlemans fellow.

[Exit **MISTRISS**.

LURCHER
Rise and be good, keep home and tend your business.

WILD-BRAIN
Thou hast don't to purpose, give me thy hand Tom;
Shall we be friends? thou seest what state I am in,
I'll undertake this pennance to my Aunt,
Just as I am, and openly I'll goe;
Where, if I be received again for currant,
And fortune smile once more—

LURCHER
Nay, nay, I'm satisfied, so farewel honest louzie Jack.

WILD-BRAIN
I cannot help it, some men meet with strange destinies.
If things go right thou mayst be hang'd, and I
May live to see't, and purchase thy apparel:
So farewel Tom, commend me to thy Polcat.

[Exit.

[Enter **LADY, NURSE, SERVANT**.

LADY
Now that I have my counsel ready, and my cause ripe;
The Judges all inform'd of the abuses;
Now that he should be gone.

NURSE
No man knows whether,
And yet they talk he went forth with a Constable
That told him of strange business that would bring him
Money and Lands, and Heaven knows what; but they
Have search'd, and cannot find out such an Officer:
And as a secret, Madam, they told your man
Nicholas, whom you sent thither as a spie,
They had a shrewd suspition 'twas the devil
I' th' likeness of a Constable, that has tempted him:
By this time to strange things; there have been men
As rich as he, have met convenient rivers,
And so forth; many trees have born strange fruits:
D'ye think he has not hang'd himself?

LADY
If he be hang'd, who has his goods?

NURSE
They are forfeited, they say.

LADY
He has hang'd himself for certain then,
Only to cosin me of my Girls portion.

NURSE
Very likely.

LADY
Or did not the Constable carry him to some prison?

NURSE
They thought on that too, and search'd every where.

LADY
He may be close for treason, perhaps executed.

NURSE
Nay, they did look among the quarters too,
And mustered all the bridge-house for his night-cap.

[Enter **SERVANT**.

SERVANT
Madam, here is the gentleman agen.

LADY
What Gentleman?

SERVANT
He that lov'd my young Mistriss.

LADY
Alas, 'tis Heartlove, 'twill but feed his melancholy.
To let him see Maria, since we dare not
Yet tell the world she lives; and certainly,
Did not the violence of his passion blind him,
He would see past her borrowed tongue and habit.

NURSE
Please you entertain him awhile, Madam,
I'll cast about for something with your daughter.

LADY
Do what thou wot, pray Mr. Heartlove enter.

[Exit **SERVANT** and **NURSE** severally.

[Enter **HEARTLOVE**.

HEARTLOVE
Madam, I come to ask your gentle pardon.

LADY
Pardon, for what? you ne'r offended me.

HEARTLOVE
Yes, if ye be the mother of Maria.

LADY
I was her mother, but that word is cancell'd,

And buried with her in that very minute
Her soul fled from her; we lost both our names
Of mother and of daughter.

HEARTLOVE
Alas, Madam,
If your relation did consist but in
Those naked terms, I had a title nearer,
Since love unites more than the tie of blood;
No matter for the empty voice of mother;
Your nature still is left, which in her absence
Must love Maria, and not see her ashes
And memory polluted.

LADY
You amaze me, by whom?

HEARTLOVE
By me, I am the vile profaner.

LADY
Why do you speak thus indiscreetly, Sir?
You ever honour'd her.

HEARTLOVE
I did a live,
But since she died, I ha been a villain to her.

LADY
I do beseech you say not so; all this
Is but to make me know how much I sinn'd
In forcing her to marry.

HEARTLOVE
Do not mock me,
I charge you by the Virgin you have wept for;
For I have done an impious act against her,
A deed able to fright her from her sleep,
And through her marble, ought to be reveng'd;
A wickedness, that if I should be silent,
You as a witness must accuse me for't.

LADY
Was I a witness?

HEARTLOVE
Yes, you knew I lov'd
Maria once; or grant, you did but think so,

By what I ha profest, or she has told you,
Was't not a fault unpardonable in me,
When I should drop my tears upon her grave,
Yes, and proof sufficient.

LADY
To what?

HEARTLOVE
That I, forgetful of my fame and vows
To fair Maria, e'r the worm could pierce
Her tender shroud, had chang'd her for another;
Did you not blush to see me turn a rebel?
So soon to court a shadow, a strange thing,
Without a name? Did you not curse my levity,
Or think upon her death with the less sorrow
That she had scap'd a punishment more killing,
Oh how I shame to think on't.

LADY
Sir, in my
Opinion, 'twas an argument of love
To your Maria, for whose sake you could
Affect one that but carried her small likeness.

HEARTLOVE
No more, you are too charitable, but
I know my guilt, and will from henceforth never
Change words with that strange maid, whose innocent face
Like your Maria's won so late upon me:
My passions are corrected, and I can
Look on her now, and woman-kind, without
Love in a thought; 'tis thus, I came to tell you,
If after this acknowledgement, you'll be
So kind to shew me in what silent grave
You have dispos'd your daughter, I will ask
Forgiveness of all her dust, and never leave,
Till with a loud confession of my shame,
I wake her ghost, and that pronounce my pardon:
Will you deny this favour? then farewel,
I'll never see you more: ha!

[Enter **NURSE, MARIA** in her own apparel, after some shew of wonder, he goes towards her.

LADY
Be not deluded, Sir, upon my life
This is the soul whom you but thought Maria
In my daughters habit; what did you mean Nurse?

I knew she would but cozen you, is she not like now?
One dew unto another is not nearer.

NURSE
She thinks she is a gentlewoman;
And that imagination has so taken her,
S h e scorns to speak, how handsomly she carries it,
As if she were a well bred thing, her body!
And I warrant you, what looks!

LADY
Pray be not foolish.

HEARTLOVE
I disturb no body, speak but half a word
And I am satisfied, but what needs that?
I'll swear 'tis she.

LADY
But do not, I beseech you,
For trust me, Sir, you know not what I know.

HEARTLOVE
Peace then,
And let me pray, she holds up her hands with me.

LADY
This will betray all.

HEARTLOVE
Love ever honor'd,
And ever young, thou Soveraign of all hearts
Of all our sorrows, the sweet ease.

[She weeps now.

Does she still cosin me?

NURSE
You will see anon,
'Twas her desire, expect the issue, Madam.

HEARTLOVE
My soul's so big, I cannot pray; 'tis she,
I will go nearer.

[Enter **ALGRIPE, LURCHER, BOY.**

NURSE
Here's Mr. Algripe, and other strangers, Madam.

ALGRIPE
Here good Lady,
Upon my knees I ask thy worships pardon;
Here's the whole summ I had with thy fair Daughter;
Would she were living, I might have her peace too,
And yield her up again to her old liberty:
I had a wife before, and could not marry;
My pennance shall be on that man that honor'd her,
To conferr some Land.

LADY
This is incredible.

ALGRIPE
'Tis truth.

LURCHER
Do you know me, Sir?

ALGRIPE
Ha, the Gentleman I deceiv'd.

LURCHER
My name is Lurcher.

ALGRIPE
'Shat have thy Mortgage.

LURCHER
I ha that already, no matter for the Deed
If you release it.

ALGRIPE
I'll do't before thy witness;
But where's thy Sister? if she live I am happy, though
I conceal our contract, which was
Stolen from me with the Evidence of this Land.

[The **BOY** goes to **MARIA**, and gives her a paper; she wonders, and smiles upon **HEARTLOVE**, he amaz'd, approaches her: afterward she shews it her **MOTHER**, and then gives it to **HEARTLOVE**.

NURSE
Your daughter smiles.

LURCHER

I hope she lives, but where, I cannot tell, Sir.

BOY
Even here, and please you, Sir.

ALGRIPE
How?

BOY
Nay, 'tis she;
To work thy fair way, I preserved you brother,
That would have lost me willingly, and serv'd ye
Thus like a boy; I served you faithfully,
And cast your plots but to preserve your credit;
Your foul ones I diverted to fair uses;
So far as you would hearken to my counsel;
That all the world may know how much you owe me.

ALGRIPE
Welcome entirely, welcome my dear Alathe,
And when I lose thee agen, blessing forsake me:
Nay, let me kiss thee in these cloaths.

LURCHER
And I too,
And bless the time I had so wise a sister, wer't thou the little thief?

BOY
I stole the contract, I must confess,
And kept it to my self, it most concern'd me.

HEARTLOVE
Contracted? this destroys his after marriage.

MARIA
Dare you give this hand
To this young Gentleman? my heart goes with it.

ALGRIPE
Maria alive! how my heart's exalted, 'tis my duty;
Take her Frank Heartlove, take her; and all joyes
With her; besides some Lands to advance her Joynture:

LADY
What I have is your own, and blessings crown ye.

HEARTLOVE
Give me room,

And fresh air to consider, Gentlemen,
My hopes are too high.

MARIA
Be more temperate,
Or I'll be Welsh again.

ALGRIPE
A day of wonder.

LURCHER
Lady, your love, I ha kept my word; there was
A time, when my much suffering made me hate you,
And to that end I did my best to cross you:
And fearing you were dead, I stole your Coffin,
That you might never more usurp my Office:
Many more knacks I did, which at the Weddings
Shall be told of as harmless tales.   Shout within.

[Enter **WILD-BRAIN**.

WILD-BRAIN
Hollow your throats apieces, I am at home;
If you can roar me out again—

LADY
What thing is this?

LURCHER
A continent of Fleas: room for the Pageant;
Make room afore there; your kinsman Madam.

LADY
My kinsman? let me wonder!

WILD-BRAIN
Do, and I'll wonder too to see this company
At peace one with another; 'tis not worth
Your admiration, I was never dead yet;
Y' re merry Aunt, I see, and all your company:
If ye be not, I'll fool up, and provoke ye:
I will do any thing to get your love again:
I'll forswear Midnight Taverns and Temptations;
Give good example to your Grooms, the Maids
Shall go to bed, and take their rest this year;
None shall appear with blisters in their bellies.

LURCHER

And when you will fool again, you may go ring.

WILD-BRAIN
Madam, have mercy.

LADY
Your submission, Sir,
I gladly take; we will
Enquire the reason of this habit afterwards;
Now you are soundly sham'd, well, we restore you
Where's Toby?
Where's the Coachman?

NURSE
He's a bed, Madam.
And has an ague, he says.

LURCHER
I'll be his Physitian.

LADY
We must afoot then.

LURCHER
E'er the Priest ha done
Toby shall wait upon you with his Coach,
And make your Flanders Mares dance back agen we'ye,
I warrant you Madam you are mortified,
Your sute shall be granted too.

WILD-BRAIN
Make, make room afore the re .

LADY
Home forward with glad hearts, home child.

MARIA
I wait you.

HEARTLOVE
On joyfully, the cure of all our grief,
Is owing to this pretty little Thief.

[Exeunt **OMNES**.

JOHN FLETCHER – A SHORT BIOGRAPHY

John Fletcher was born in December, 1579 in Rye, Sussex. He was baptised on December 20th.

As can be imagined details of much of his life and career have not survived and, accordingly, only a very brief indication of his life and works can be given.

His father, Richard Fletcher, was a successful and rather ambitious cleric. From being the Dean of Peterborough he moved on to become the Bishop of Bristol, Bishop of Worcester and finally, shortly before his death, the Bishop of London. He was also the chaplain to Queen Elizabeth.

When he was Dean of Peterborough, Richard Fletcher, witnessed the execution of Mary, Queen of Scots. It was said he "knelt down on the scaffold steps and started to pray out loud and at length, in a prolonged and rhetorical style, as though determined to force his way into the pages of history". He cried out at her death, "So perish all the Queen's enemies!" All very dramatic but the family did have strong links to the Arts.

Young Fletcher appears at the very young age of eleven to have entered Corpus Christi College at Cambridge University in 1591. There are no records that he ever took a degree but there is some small evidence that he was being prepared for a career in the church.

However what is clear is that this was soon abandoned as he joined the stream of people who would leave University and decamp to the more bohemian life of commercial theatre in London.

Unfortunately his father fell out with Queen Elizabeth but appears to have been on his way to rehabilitation before his death in 1596. At his death he was, however, mired in debt.

The upbringing of the now teenage Fletcher and his seven siblings now passed to his paternal uncle, the poet and minor official Giles Fletcher. Giles, who had the patronage of the Earl of Essex may have been a liability rather than an advantage to the young Fletcher. With Essex involved in the failed rebellion against Elizabeth Giles was also tainted by association.

By 1606 John Fletcher appears to have equipped himself with the talents to become a playwright. Initially this appears to have been for the Children of the Queen's Revels, then performing at the Blackfriars Theatre.

Commendatory verses by Richard Brome in the Beaumont and Fletcher 1647 folio place Fletcher in the company of Ben Jonson, although it is not known when this friendship began. Jonson, of course, was a leviathan of English Literature, so admired that many of his literary friends and colleagues were simply known as 'Sons of Ben'. Fletcher's frequent early collaborator, Francis Beaumont, was also a friend of Jonson's.

Fletcher's early career was marked by one significant failure; The Faithful Shepherdess, his adaptation of Giovanni Battista Guarini's Il Pastor Fido, which was performed by the Blackfriars Children in 1608. In the preface to the printed edition of his play, Fletcher explained the failure as due to his audience's faulty expectations. They expected a pastoral tragicomedy to feature dances, comedy, and murder, with the shepherds presented in conventional stereotypes – as Fletcher put it, wearing "gray cloaks, with curtailed dogs in strings." Fletcher's preface is however best known for its pithy definition of tragicomedy: "A tragicomedy is not so called in respect of mirth and killing, but in respect it wants [i.e., lacks] deaths, which is enough to make it no tragedy; yet brings some near it, which is enough to make it no comedy." A comedy, he went on to say, must be "a representation of familiar people." His preface is critical of drama that features characters whose action violates nature.

In that case, Fletcher appears to have been developing a new style faster than audiences could comprehend. By 1609, however, he had found his stride. With Beaumont, he wrote Philaster, which became a hit for the King's Men and began a profitable association between Fletcher and that company. Philaster appears also to have begun a trend for tragicomedy. Fletcher's influence has also been said to have inspired some features of Shakespeare's late romances, and certainly his influence on the tragicomic work of other playwrights is even more marked.

By the middle of the 1610s, Fletcher's plays had achieved a popularity that rivalled Shakespeare's and cemented the pre-eminence of the King's Men in Jacobean London. After Beaumont's retirement, necessitated by ill-health, and then his early death in 1616, Fletcher continued working, both singly and in collaboration, until his death in 1625. By that time, he had produced, or had been credited with, close to fifty plays. This body of work remained a major part of the King's Men's repertory until the closing of the theatres in 1642 due to the Civil War.

At the beginning of his career Fletcher's most important collaborator was Francis Beaumont. The two wrote together for close to a decade, first for the Children of the Queen's Revels, and then for the King's Men. According to an anecdote transmitted or invented by John Aubrey, they also lived together in Bankside, sharing clothes and having "one wench in the house between them." This domestic arrangement, if it existed, was ended by Beaumont's marriage in 1613, and their dramatic partnership ended after Beaumont fell ill, probably of a stroke, that same year.

At this point Fletcher had written many plays with Beaumont and several others on his own. He seems to have been regarded as quite a talent although it should be remembered that playwrights were required to be prolific, to easily work with other collaborators and to produce work of quality and commercial appeal very quickly.

The King's Men, run by Philip Henslowe, was the most prestigious of the theatre companies and Fletcher now had an increasingly close association with it.

Fletcher collaborated with Shakespeare on Henry VIII, The Two Noble Kinsmen, and the now lost Cardenio, which some scholars say was the basis for Lewis Theobald's play Double Falsehood. (Theobald is regarded as one of the best Shakespearean editors. Whether his play is based on Cardenio or on some other is not absolutely known although Theobald certainly promoted it as his revision of the lost Shakespeare/Fletcher play.)

A play that Fletcher also wrote by himself at this time, The Woman's Prize or the Tamer Tamed, is also regarded as a sequel to The Taming of the Shrew.

In 1616, with the death of Shakespeare, Fletcher now appears to have entered into an enhanced arrangement with the King's Men on very similar terms to Shakespeare's. Fletcher would now write exclusively for the King's Men until his own death almost a decade later.

As well as continuing his solo productions Fletcher was still collaborating with other playwrights, mainly Philip Massinger, who, in turn, would succeed him as the in-house playwright for the King's Men.

Fletcher's popularity continued throughout his life; indeed during the winter of 1621, he had three of his plays performed at court. His mastery is most notable in two dramatic types; tragicomedy and the comedy of manners.

John Fletcher died in 1625, it is thought of bubonic plague which, at the time, was undergoing further outbreaks.

He seems to have been buried in what is now Southwark Cathedral, although a precise location is not known. There is much made of an anecdote that Fletcher and Massinger (who died in 1640) share the same grave but it is more likely that both are buried within a few yards of each other and that the stone markers in the floor have confused the issue. One is marked 'Edmond Shakespeare 1607' and the other 'John Fletcher 1625' refers to Shakespeare's younger brother and the playwright. The churchyards were, more often than not, completely over-crowded and breeding grounds for disease. Precise record keeping was not a practiced skill.

During the later Commonwealth, many of the playwright's best-known scenes were kept alive as drolls. These were brief performances, usually condensed into one or two scenes and with the addition of music or song to satisfy the taste for plays while the theatres were closed under the Puritans. At the re-opening of the theatres in 1660, the plays in the Fletcher canon, in original form or revised, were by far the most common productions on the English stage. The most frequently revived plays suggest the developing taste for comedies of manners. Among the tragedies, The Maid's Tragedy and, especially, Rollo Duke of Normandy held the stage. Four tragicomedies (A King and No King, The Humorous Lieutenant, Philaster, and The Island Princess) were popular, perhaps in part for their similarity to and foreshadowing of heroic drama. Four comedies (Rule a Wife And Have a Wife, The Chances, Beggars' Bush, and especially The Scornful Lady) were also stage mainstays.

Despite his popularity, and it appears he was held in higher regard than Shakespeare at this time, his works steadily lost ground to those of Shakespeare and to new productions from other playwrights.

Since then Fletcher has increasingly become a subject only for occasional revivals and for specialists. Fletcher and his collaborators have been the subject of important bibliographic and critical studies, but the plays have been revived only infrequently.

Due to the frequent collaborations between all manner of playwrights, and the revisions carried out in later years, having a settled list of authorship to any given set of plays can be problematic. The works of Fletcher and others of this period most definitely fall into this category. It is as well to take into account that during this period theatres were quite often closed either due to outbreaks of the plague or to the prevailing political and moral climate. Printers, anxious to provide materials that would sell, were not above changing a name or two to enhance sales.

Although Fletcher collaborated most often with Beaumont and Massinger, it is believed that Massinger revised many of the plays some time after their original production. Other collaborators including Nathan Field, William Shakespeare, William Rowley and others also can be seen distinctly in Fletchers' works. Many modern scholars point out that Fletcher had many particular mannerisms but other playwrights would also duplicate these at times so allocating exact contributions of anyone to a play is somewhat of a detective case in many instances. However from the original folio printings or licensing via the Master of the Revels (the statutory licensing authority to approve and censor plays as well a hand in publication and printing of theatrical materials) as well as contemporary notes a fairly precise bibliography of the works can be given with only a few plays lacking substantial authority and provenance.

JOHN FLETCHER – A CONCISE BIBLIOGRAPHY

This bibliography gives the most likely date of writing together with when published, revised or licensed by the Master or the Revels (This position within the royal household was originally for royal festivities, ie revels, and later to oversee stage censorship, until this function was transferred to the Lord Chamberlain in 1624).

Solo Plays
The Faithful Shepherdess, pastoral (written 1608–9; printed 1609)
The Tragedy of Valentinian, tragedy (1610–14; 1647)
Monsieur Thomas, comedy (c. 1610–16; 1639)
The Woman's Prize, or The Tamer Tamed, comedy (c. 1611; 1647)
Bonduca, tragedy (1611–14; 1647)
The Chances, comedy (c. 1613–25; 1647)
Wit Without Money, comedy (c. 1614; 1639)
The Mad Lover, tragicomedy (acted 5 January 1617; 1647)
The Loyal Subject, tragicomedy (licensed 16 November 1618; revised 1633; 1647)
The Humorous Lieutenant, tragicomedy (c. 1619; 1647)
Women Pleased, tragicomedy (c. 1619–23; 1647)
The Island Princess, tragicomedy (c. 1620; 1647)
The Wild Goose Chase, comedy (c. 1621; 1652)
The Pilgrim, comedy (c. 1621; 1647)
A Wife for a Month, tragicomedy (licensed 27 May 1624; 1647)
Rule a Wife and Have a Wife, comedy (licensed 19 October 1624; 1640)

Collaborations

With Francis Beaumont
The Woman Hater, comedy (1606; 1607)
Cupid's Revenge, tragedy (c. 1607–12; 1615)
Philaster, or Love Lies a-Bleeding, tragicomedy (c. 1609; 1620)
The Maid's Tragedy, Tragedy (c. 1609; 1619)
A King and No King, tragicomedy (1611; 1619)
The Captain, comedy (c. 1609–12; 1647)
The Scornful Lady, comedy (c. 1613; 1616)
Love's Pilgrimage, tragicomedy (c. 1615–16; 1647)
The Noble Gentleman, comedy (c. 1613; licensed 3 February 1626; 1647)

With Francis Beaumont & Philip Massinger
Thierry & Theodoret, tragedy (c. 1607; 1621)
The Coxcomb, comedy (c. 1608–10; 1647)

Beggars' Bush, comedy (c. 1612–13; revised 1622; 1647)
Love's Cure, comedy (c. 1612–13; revised 1625; 1647)

With Philip Massinger
Sir John van Olden Barnavelt, tragedy (August 1619; MS)
The Little French Lawyer, comedy (c. 1619–23; 1647)
A Very Woman, tragicomedy (c. 1619–22; licensed 6 June 1634; 1655)
The Custom of the Country, comedy (c. 1619–23; 1647)
The Double Marriage, tragedy (c. 1619–23; 1647)
The False One, history (c. 1619–23; 1647)
The Prophetess, tragicomedy (licensed 14 May 1622; 1647)
The Sea Voyage, comedy (licensed 22 June 1622; 1647)
The Spanish Curate, comedy (licensed 24 October 1622; 1647)
The Lovers' Progress or The Wandering Lovers, tragicomedy (licensed 6 December 1623; rev 1634; 1647)
The Elder Brother, comedy (c. 1625; 1637)

With Philip Massinger & Nathan Field
The Honest Man's Fortune, tragicomedy (1613; 1647)
The Queen of Corinth, tragicomedy (c. 1616–18; 1647)
The Knight of Malta, tragicomedy (c. 1619; 1647)

With William Shakespeare
Henry VIII, history (c. 1613; 1623)
The Two Noble Kinsmen, tragicomedy (c. 1613; 1634)
Cardenio, tragicomedy (c. 1613)

With Thomas Middleton & William Rowley
Wit at Several Weapons, comedy (c. 1610–20; 1647)

With William Rowley
The Maid in the Mill (licensed 29 August 1623; 1647).

With Nathan Field
Four Plays, or Moral Representations, in One, morality (c. 1608–13; 1647)

With Philip Massinger, Ben Jonson and George Chapman
Rollo Duke of Normandy, or The Bloody Brother, tragedy (c. 1617; revised 1627–30; 1639)

With James Shirley
The Night Walker, or The Little Thief, comedy (c. 1611; 1640)
The Coronation c. 1635

Uncertain
The Nice Valour, or The Passionate Madman, comedy (c. 1615–25; 1647)
The Laws of Candy, tragicomedy (c. 1619–23; 1647)
The Fair Maid of the Inn, comedy (licensed 22 January 1626; 1647)
The Faithful Friends, tragicomedy (registered 29 June 1660; MS.)

The Nice Valour is possibly by Fletcher revised by Thomas Middleton;

The Fair Maid of the Inn is perhaps a play by Massinger, John Ford, and John Webster, either with or without Fletcher's involvement.

The Laws of Candy has been variously attributed to Fletcher and to John Ford but the primary authorship now rests with the latter.

The Night-Walker was a Fletcher original, with additions by Shirley for a 1639 production.

Even now there is not absolute certainty on several of the plays. The first Beaumont & Fletcher folio of 1647 contained 35 plays and the second folio of 1679 added a further 18. In total 53 plays.

The first folio included The Masque of the Inner Temple and Gray's Inn (1613), and the second The Knight of the Burning Pestle (1607), widely considered Beaumont's solo works, although the latter was in early editions attributed to both writers. Fletcher himself said that Beaumont was attributed so-authorship of many works that belonged solely to Fletcher or to other collaborators.

One play in the canon, Sir John Van Olden Barnavelt, existed in manuscript and was not published till 1883.

JAMES SHIRLEY – A SHORT BIOGRAPHY

James Shirley was born in London in September 1596.

His education was through a collection of England's finest establishments: Merchant Taylors' School, London, St John's College, Oxford, and St Catharine's College, Cambridge, where he took his B.A. degree in approximately 1618.

He first published in 1618, a poem entitled Echo, or the Unfortunate Lovers.

As with many artists of this period full details of his life and career are not recorded. Sources say that after graduating he became "a minister of God's word in or near St Albans." A conversion to the Catholic faith enabled him to become master of St Albans School from 1623–25.

He wrote his first play, Love Tricks, or the School of Complement, which was licensed on February 10th, 1625. From the given date it would seem he wrote this whilst at St Albans but, after its production, he moved to London and to live in Gray's Inn.

For the next two decades, he would write prolifically and with great quality, across a spectrum of thirty plays; through tragedies and comedies to tragicomedies as well as several books of poetry. Unfortunately, his talents were left to wither when Parliament passed the Puritan edict in 1642, forbidding all stage plays and closing the theatres.

Most of his early plays were performed by Queen Henrietta's Men, the acting company for which Shirley was engaged as house dramatist.

Shirley's sympathies lay with the King in battles with Parliament and he received marks of special favor from the Queen.

He made a bitter attack on William Prynne, who had attacked the stage in Histriomastix, and, when in 1634 a special masque was presented at Whitehall by the gentlemen of the Inns of Court as a practical reply to Prynne, Shirley wrote the text—The Triumph of Peace.

Shirley spent the years 1636 to 1640 in Ireland, under the patronage of the Earl of Kildare. Several of his plays were produced by his friend John Ogilby in Dublin in the first ever constructed Irish theatre; The Werburgh Street Theatre. During his years in Dublin he wrote The Doubtful Heir, The Royal Master, The Constant Maid, and St. Patrick for Ireland.

In his absence from London, Queen Henrietta's Men sold off a dozen of his plays to the stationers, who naturally, enough published them. When Shirley returned to London in 1640, he finished with the Queen Henrietta's company and his final plays in London were acted by the King's Men.

On the outbreak of the English Civil War Shirley served with the Earl of Newcastle. However when the King's fortunes began to decline he returned to London. There his friend Thomas Stanley gave him help and thereafter Shirley supported himself in the main by teaching and publishing some educational works under the Commonwealth. In addition to these he published during the period of dramatic eclipse four small volumes of poems and plays, in 1646, 1653, 1655, and 1659.

It is said that he was "a drudge" for John Ogilby in his translations of Homer's Iliad and the Odyssey, and survived into the reign of Charles II, but, though some of his comedies were revived, his days as a playwright were over.

His death, at age seventy, along with that of his wife, in 1666, is described as one of fright and exposure due to the Great Fire of London which had raged through parts of London from September 2nd to the 5th.

He was buried at St Giles in the Fields, in London, on October 29th, 1666.

JAMES SHIRLEY – A CONCISE BIBLIOGRAPHY

The following includes years of first publication, and of performance if known, together with dates of licensing by the Master of the Revels if available.

TRAGEDIES
The Maid's Revenge (licensed 9th February 1626; printed, 1639)
The Traitor (licensed 4th May 1631; printed, 1635)
Love's Cruelty (licensed 14th November 1631; printed, 1640)
The Politician (acted, 1639; printed, 1655)
The Cardinal (licensed 25th May 1641; printed, 1652).

TRAGI-COMEDIES
The Grateful Servant (licensed 3rd November 1629 as The Faithful Servant; printed 1630)

The Young Admiral (licensed 3rd July 1633; printed 1637)
The Coronation (licensed 6th February 1635, as Shirley's, but printed in 1640 as a work of John Fletcher)
The Duke's Mistress (licensed 18th January 1636; printed 1638)
The Gentleman of Venice (licensed 30th October 1639; printed 1655)
The Doubtful Heir (printed 1652), licensed as Rosania, or Love's Victory in 1640
The Imposture (licensed 10th November 1640; printed 1652)
The Court Secret (printed 1653).

COMEDIES

Love Tricks, or the School of Complement (licensed 10th February 1625; printed under its subtitle, 1631)
The Wedding (ca. 1626; printed 1629)
The Brothers (licensed 4th November 1626; printed 1652)
The Witty Fair One (licensed 3rd October 1628; printed 1633)
The Humorous Courtier (licensed 17th May 1631; printed 1640).
The Changes, or Love in a Maze (licensed 10th January 1632; printed 1639)
Hyde Park (licensed 20th April 1632; printed 1637)
The Ball (licensed 16th November 1632; printed 1639)
The Bird in a Cage, or The Beauties (licensed 21st January 1633; printed 1633)
The Gamester (licensed 11th November 1633; printed 1637)
The Example (licensed 24th June 1634; printed 1637)
The Opportunity (licensed 29th November 1634; printed 1640)
The Lady of Pleasure (licensed 15th October 1635; printed 1637)
The Royal Master (acted and printed 1638)
The Constant Maid, or Love Will Find Out the Way (printed 1640)
The Sisters (licensed 26th April 1642; printed 1653).
Honoria and Mammon (printed 1659)

DRAMAS

A Contention for Honor and Riches (printed 1633), morality play
The Triumph of Peace (licensed 3rd February 1634; printed 1634), masque
The Arcadia (printed 1640), pastoral tragicomedy
St. Patrick for Ireland (printed 1640), neo-miracle play
The Triumph of Beauty (ca. 1640; printed 1646), masque
The Contention of Ajax and Ulysses (printed 1659), entertainment
Cupid and Death (performed 26th March 1653; printed 1659), masque

www.ingramcontent.com/pod-product-compliance
Lightning Source LLC
Chambersburg PA
CBHW060116050426
42448CB00010B/1898